The Health Spas

Note: The information in this book is presented for general interest only and not to suggest medical treatment of any kind in any particular case. Such advice should be obtained from your professional health counsellor.

It is suggested that the reader communicate directly with any establishment in which he is interested to determine its current status, program, and availability. Because of the wide range of information contained in the book, and because changes do occur, accuracy in each detail cannot be guaranteed.

The Health Spas

A world guidebook to
Health Spas and Nature-Cure Centers
. . . all the best places for rest and rejuvenation

By Robert and Raye Yaller

With a foreword by
Paavo O. Airola, Ph.D.

A Lifeline Book
™

Published by
Woodbridge Press Publishing Company
Santa Barbara, California 93111

A Lifeline Book

Published by
Woodbridge Press Publishing Company
Post Office Box 6189
Santa Barbara, California 93111

Library of Congress Catalog Card Number: 74-21128

International Standard Book Number: 0-912800-10-0

Published simultaneously in the United States and Canada

Printed in the United States of America

Dedication

This book is dedicated to Dr. Bess S. Gorman, D.C., our friend and teacher. She has helped us to understand that there are no shortcuts to optimum health. To win it is the work of a lifetime and the promotion of it is a branch of preventive medicine.

Contents

Part III: *A World Guide To Health Spas*

Part IV: *Some Special Information*

Dramatic Results
Are Possible

A foreword by

Paavo O. Airola, Ph.D.

Hot mineral waters and spas have helped to keep inhabitants of this planet healthy and fit for thousands of years; but, somehow, they fell into disrepute early in this "scientific" twentieth century. Modern, drug-oriented medicine had no place in its arsenal of treatments for nature-cure methods — mineral waters and other drugless naturopathic therapies — which were branded as superstitious quackery.

However, rapid changes are now taking place in the attitude of orthodox medicine towards nature-cure spas. It can be rightfully said that health spas, mineral baths, and nature-cure (biological) clinics are enjoying an unprecedented renaissance.

Although the United States is lagging behind in this field, health spas are accepted and officially sanctioned institutions in most countries, particularly in Europe. Millions of people visit such spas both for prophylactic and therapeutic purposes.

The authors of this guidebook can be congratulated for their excellent presentation of selected nature-cure spas in many of the countries they have visited. Their information is authentic, reliable, and timely.

There is a crying need for such a book. It will help many health seekers who, disappointed by the failure of a conventional medical approach to solve their health problems, wish to find a place where they can let nature and harmless, drugless naturopathic methods help to restore their health.

I have had the privilege of studying in several spas and nature-cure clinics in Europe. I have also had personal experience with spa work while directing a biological clinic in Mexico for several years.

Thus, I can testify that spa treatments, as described herein, including fasting, mineral waters and other hydrotherapies, massage, rest, raw juices and special therapeutic diets, can indeed produce dramatic results towards the restoration and maintenance of good health.

— Paavo O. Airola, Ph.D.

Part I
An Introduction To Spas

Nutrition, rest, exercise, waters, therapies

He who has health has hope
And he who has hope has everything

— *Arabian proverb*

Why Millions Visit the Spas for Renewed Health

Why do millions of people all over the world visit the health spas and nature-cure clinics — biological clinics? We believe it is because there is a growing awareness of the need to build good health — not merely to treat disease — as well as an awareness of the failure of traditional medical practice to cure many illnesses — and of the dangerous side effects of many so-called wonder drugs used in conventional medical practice.

Our present-day health statistics are disconcerting to say the least. Half of the United States population may be regarded as chronically ill, according to a 1971 report of the World Health Organization. Of 225 reporting countries, the United States was 99th in terms of its death rate. Some of the poorest countries in the world have lower death rates than the United States.

The WHO report indicated that the United States had 23 million persons with heart disease, 20 million suffering from mental illness, 20 million persons with high blood pressure, 14 million with low blood pressure. There are 9 million alcoholics, 12 million with anemia, 6 million suffering from arthritis, and 5.5 million with some form of visual impairment. One of every 6 Americans will die from cancer.

13

But for thousands of years spas have contributed to the prevention of disease, to the improvement and healing of chronic conditions, and to the restoration of health for millions all over the world.

In every ancient culture there are stories of healing by mineral waters. Indians wandered thru the Mojave Desert in the Southwest until they found hot mineral springs for drinking and bathing. European countries have a 2,000-year tradition of spa treatment. The Romans restored their battle-scarred bodies in hot mineral springs.

The natural qualities of such springs and the usually favorable climatic conditions seem to act upon affected organs, the involuntary nervous system, and the endocrine glands — all vital for the prevention of disease. Spa therapy does aid in the regeneration of the body.

Some physiologists suggest that certain vital organs of the body have phenomemal endurance, that the liver and the heart, for example, should last — with proper care — from 150 to 200 years. And, indeed, there are enough examples of great longevity to encourage us all. The Soviet Union (with more than 3,500 spas, incidentally) has more than 12,000 people who are over 110 years of age. The founder of Glasgow Cathedral lived to the age of 185. Thomas Carn, born January 25, 1588, died in 1795.His age: 207 years, according to records in London. Janus Rowen, a Hungarian, lived to be 172; his widqw died at 164; their son passed away at 115.

We believe that spas can help you prolong your life. Since 1955, we have been visiting health resorts, and nature-cure spas (biological clinics) in the United States, Mexico, Europe, the Soviet Union, Israel and elsewhere. We were staff members for a year at the largest health resort in North America — Rancho La Puerta, in Mexico. We have taken the waters at many of the spas we have visited.

There are thousands of spas all over the world. In this book we list many of them but must limit detailed descriptions to those we have visited.

Different countries have different names for their spas: nature-cure spas, Kurorte, health resorts, health farms, health schools, Heilbader, hydros, holiday health centers, stations thermales, beauty farms, biological clinics, health reconditioning centers, sanatoria, etc., but almost all work on similar principles.

In Europe, crenotherapy (from *krene*, Greek for mineral spring) is a science with many well-developed branches and an important part of the official health services of many countries.

There are strict laws governing European national spas and the therapies they apply. Only scientifically tested remedies are recognized and approved. Spas are examined regularly and the required standards maintained. In the larger spas of the Soviet Union there are research institutes, generally attached to a university, where there is continous research in order to bring about beneficial results.

The basis for most spa therapy is naturopathy. It is based on the integrity of the body: find the cause of the illness, eliminate it, and the body will heal itself. Naturopathy (healing without drugs or surgery) has placed at our dissposal a wide range of remedies offering many possibilities for restoring and maintaining good health. These include proper nutrition, fasting, hydrotherapy, electrotherapy, massage, high colonics, fresh air, sunshine, recreation, rest, pleasant surroundings, and exercise.

A modern thermal pool

A healthy body is the guest chamber
of the soul; a sick one its prison

— *Francis Bacon*

All Spas
Are Not Alike

There are three main types of resorts for the health seeker:
    Nature-cure spas (biological clinics)
    Sanatoria
        a. Inpatient
        b. Outpatient
    Health resorts (holiday centers or vacation houses)

Nature-cure spas base their therapies on the belief that the body must build up its own resistance to diseases and not rely on surgery or synthetic drugs. Only natural remedies are used at these spas with emphasis on fasting, proper nutrition, natural herbs, vitamins, etc. Since constant care and supervision are required in this type of therapy, these institutions are usually small and accommodate a limited number of patients.

Some of the outstanding nature-cure spas where these methods are followed are:
    Bircher-Benner Clinic, *Zurich, Switzerland*
    Enton Hall, *Godalming, Surrey, England*
    Vita Dell Spa, *Desert Hot Springs, California*
    Meadowlark Spa, *Hemet, California*

Orange Grove Health Ranch, *Arcadia, Florida*
Bay N' Gulf, *St. Petersburg, Florida*
Dr. Shelton's Health School, *San Antonio, Texas*
Florida Spa, *Orlando, Florida*
Villa Vegetariana, *Cuernavaca, Mexico*
Dr. Esser's Health Ranch, *Lake Worth, Florida*

A *sanatorium* is a place to which those who are suffering from mental or physical problems go for specific tratments. Emphasis is on hydrotherapy. Hundreds of patients are treated in sometimes very large establishments. The two types of sanatoria are:
Inpatient. The guests reside in a large hotel where therapy facilities are located. Diets are prescribed and food is taken in a special dining room. Some of the most outstanding are:
Marienbad (Marianske Lazne and Carlsbad — Karlovy Vary), *Czechoslovakia*
Bad Elster, Bad Brambach, Potsdam Neufahrland Diet Sanatorium, *East Germany*
Vichy, *France*
Sochi, *USSR*
Outpatient. The guests are housed in many hotels, pensions, rooms, etc. They take their meals wherever they choose. Daily they go to a large establishment where all the various therapies are concentrated. Among the outpatient centers are:
Baden-Baden, Wiesbaden, and Bad Nauheim, *West Germany*
Aix-les-Bains, Aix-en-Provence, *France*
Royal Leamington Spa, Bath, *England*
Salzburg Therapeutic Center, *Austria*

Health resorts are generally for basically healthy people who wish to maintain physical fitness and prevent the development of health problems. These resorts are health-oriented, providing many beneficial facilities such as a swimming pool, a gymnasium, a solarium (for nude sunbathing), etc. They also place special emphasis on good nutrition, fruits and vegetables — organically grown in some cases. They avoid white sugar, white flour, coffee, pastries and all similarly devitalized or harmful products.

In the category of health resorts are:

Rancho La Puerta and Rio Caliente, *Mexico*

Jacumba Hot Springs and the Golden Door, *California*

Almost all nature-cure spas, sanatoria, and health resorts welcome guests who are healthy and wish to remain so. They need not necessarily apply for any kind of treatments. In this sense all spas are health resorts.

You don't have to be ill to enjoy a spa. Prevention is much better than cure. Health-minded vacationers can profit by a three or four week stay at any spa of their choice. There is no better way to stay well.

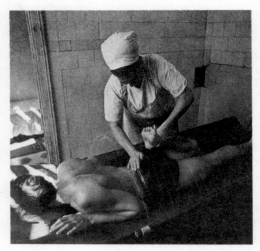

Waters and massage

Special sprays and showers

Sickness is the retribution
of an outraged nature

The Nature–Cure Way
To Longer Life

Nature-cure spas base their therapies in general on the philosophy of naturopathy (natural healing). This philosophy declares that much acute disease is nature's way of eliminating waste matter in the tissues of the body. It is based on the principle that within the organism itself lies the essential healing force for overcoming disease. The body builds up its own resistance to disease. Surgery or synthetic drugs, it is believed, remove the symptoms without revealing the basic cause. A specific drug against a specific organism becomes an almost impossible search, since organisms tend to become resistant to drugs. Generally, only natural remedies are applied at nature-cure spas.

The first step in effecting a cure is the restoration of normal body functions. To help release the body's own forces of healing, there are natural procedures which include therapeutic fasting, proper nutrition, hydrotherapy, osteopathic and chiropractic procedures, high colonics, electrotherapy, exercise, air, sunbathing, vigorous walking, rest, recreation, psychological counseling, etc.

In most spas the essence of treatment is in hydrotherapy,

the scientific use of water. It is used for bathing, drinking, internal use, and for inhalation as vapor.

Dr. Leo Hruby, director of Carlsbad (Karlovy Vary) in Czechoslovakia, gives the following clinical report on how mineral waters help the patient.

"The effects of the mineral waters are twofold: on the one hand they influence directly the digestive organs such as the mucous membranes of the stomach; on the other hand, the water is absorbed by the organism, led through the liver into the blood circulation and afterwards eliminated through the kidneys. Thus the water introduces various salts into the organism in a perfectly balanced composition. This internal effect of the cure has a very favorable effect upon the reduction of the inflammatory process.

"The skin is a body organ having great influence upon one's health. It carries nearly one-third of all the blood in the body and can bring about good or bad effects on the blood stream. It acts as a temperature regulator for the body. The 2.5 million sweat glands in the skin eliminate much of the body waste that is always passing out of one's system.

"Many diseases result from the skin's sensitivity to external changes of heat and cold. Hydrotherapy helps the skin to adapt itself to these changes. Mineral waters stimulate the natural action of the skin to improve circulation and to tone up muscles and tissue."

The therapeutic value of hydrotherapy is said to be enhanced by the following mineral properties of various waters.

Iodine springs get good results in high blood pressure, in various types of eye diseases, in chronic inflammation of the female organs, and in circulatory problems.

Iron springs help in iron deficiency.

Sodium chloride waters are used to correct functional disorders of the circulation and women's diseases.

Sulphur springs are most helpful for rheumatic problems, metabolic disorders, and skin diseases.

Springs with radon content are known for the alleviation of pain. They help to correct disturbances of the endocrine glands. They stimulate metabolism in all of the cells and they reduce inflammation of the nerves.

Acidulous waters act favorably upon heart muscles that may have been damaged by overindulgence in alcohol and smoking. They give new elasticity to the heart and improve circulation. These waters are also prescribed for the drinking cure, in disorders of the gastrointestinal tract, in urological diseases for steam inhalation and for chronic catarrhs of the upper respiratory tract.

Glauber salt springs promote the production of bile and its evacuation into the intestines and bring back the elasticity of the gall bladder. They also help in diseases of obesity, diabetes and gout.

Exercise is widely used in health spas. It is absolutely essential to health. Constructive exercise loosens the debris accumulating in the tissues and develops muscles and maintains their elasticity. It improves circulation and breaks down fatty deposits and increases elimination. It stimulates cell activity and circulation of the blood. Suitable and individual remedial exercises are given in spas for patients who need special attention to build up any particular organ or tissue.

Osteopathic and chiropractic procedures serve to loosen the muscles and joints and to correct bad posture and other abnormalities of the body structure.

High colonics cleanse the colon and aid in peristaltic action.

Proper nutrition is basic to all spa treatment. Food may cause or cure disease, depending upon its origin, composition, and the manner in which it is prepared and consumed. Fresh, unspoiled greens from healthy soil have unequaled health-promoting power. Food *is* your best medicine. An Egyptian doctor wrote more than 3,600 years ago, "Man eats too much, lives on one-fourth of all he is eating, and the remaining three-fourths serve as a livelihood for the physicians."

So you can see that modes of therapy and health maintenance at health spas and nature-cure clinics are greatly varied. The study of such methods has become a science in many countries and they are being used with increasing precision and effectiveness.

Part II
Special Kinds of Spas

The Buchinger Sanatorium

He who would eat much must eat little
For by eating less he will live longer
And so be able to eat more

— *Luigi Cornaro, Padua, 1538*

Fast
Your Way To Health

Can fasting and eating both be effective ways to renewed health? Yes; and both are utilized in the therapy offered at various nature-cure clinics. In this chapter we describe several establishments that have well-developed plans for supervised fasting therapy.

Buchinger Sanatorium for Biological Therapy

Supervised fasting is the best therapy to restore one's physical and mental health, according to Dr. Otto H. F. Buchinger, director of the Buchinger Sanatorium for Biological Therapy, Bad Pyrmont, Germany.

Since 1920 the institution has kept detailed records of more than 50,000 fasting patients. Scientists have hailed the sanatorium as one of the outstanding organizations dedicated to successfully treating many diseases.

The institute has maintained for more than 50 years that properly supervised fasting therapy can produce a deep-reaching change in man's total organism and greatly accelerate the restoration of good health.

Numerous scientific articles suggest that sustained, methodical fasting, under the guidance of an experienced practioner can be the means of rejuvenating the heart and circulation.

The preventive fast seems ideally suited for a cleansing of the whole body. It does not damage nerve or vital organs, Dr. Buchinger contends; and, in fact, a majority of acute and chronic ailments can be improved or even cured by the fast.

Although the fast has been the principal therapy of the Buchinger Sanatorium since 1920, each type of treatment is prescribed according to the individual needs of patients. Seventy-five per cent of them fast, the others follow a diet therapy.

The fast is supplemented by several auxiliary therapies, including dry and underwater massages, arm and leg baths, medical baths, and sometimes psychotherapy.

Four times a week, the medical director gives informal talks and answers questions of the patients on such topics as health, homeopathy, nutrition — balanced living as well as mental health.

Many people consider fasting dangerous. However, Dr. Buchinger's experience in thousands of cases suggests that controlled fasting gives new vitality and energy to the patient. Under the ideal conditions provided in the sanatorium, fasting is not a difficult or trying experience. Some patients continue normal activities during a fast, while others benefit by a rest in bed. No one fasts unless he wants to.

The sanatorium, set in spacious, wooded grounds, is equipped to accommodate 75 patients at one time. There are gymnastic facilities and an excellent enclosed swimming pool as well as a large auditorium for cultural and social events.

Here are the techniques used for fasting at the Buchinger Sanatorium:

The first day of treatment consists of a diet of raw fruits. The three meals of fruit (about two pounds) are chosen from apples, pears, oranges, figs, prunes, etc. The fruit diet is designed to flush out quantities of fluid retained in the body.

On the following day, the patient is weighed and is interviewed by the physician assigned to his treatment. He makes a record of the patient's complete medical history;

the condition of the heart; the size and sensitivity to pressure of the liver; and the tactile findings of organs in the abdominal cavity. There is also an examination of the extremities, of the joints and the nerve reflexes, and a laboratory test of the blood and urine.

Then the patient receives about 1.5 ounces of Glauber salt in 1.25 pints of warm water as a purgative, with a small glass of orange juice to counteract its bitter taste. After the bowel cleansing, the patient gets a cup of peppermint tea.

The patient takes an enema every second day to continue the cleansing process. Each time this is followed by a cup of camomile or peppermint tea. At 11 o'clock each morning the patient gets a glass of freshly pressed, clear fruit or vegetable juice; or a cup of hot, clear, fresh vegetable broth. In the evening, there is either herb tea or grape juice.

Doctor and patient see each other daily and psychotherapy is applied when necessary. There is thus a close supervision of the treatment. Each morning, those who are able have an hour of gymnastics under medical supervision. The remaining hours are used for various other therapies.

There are two and one half to three hours of daily rest during which liver packs are applied. These stimulate the activity the liver, for this detoxification organ is said to work harder during the fast than at any other time. The organ receives an added influx of blood during this wet warm pack.

Except during the treatments, very few patients remain in bed. Even on rainy days, most are encouraged to go walking for an hour or two — both in the morning and in the afternoon. In the evenings there may be lectures on health, concerts or motion pictures, and other programs.

Dr. Buchinger cautions that it is not advisable to combine fasting and work for longer than one week because of a decreasing ability to concentrate.

Breaking the fast must be carefully supervised. On the morning the fast is broken, Dr. Buchinger prescribes two fresh apples which the patient must chew very slowly. No liquid drink is to be taken at this time. After his afternoon rest, the patient may have a cup of herb tea. In the evening a large bowl of vegetable soup is served.

The first spontaneous evacuation comes generally on the third or fourth day after eating has been resumed. There is then a final careful examination and the patient may return home with individual instructions for nutrition as well as special recommendations that will help him to retain the good health he has worked so hard to achieve.

It is strongly advised not to attempt a prolonged fast without the supervision of an experienced practitioner.

For the past 50 years the Buchinger Sanatorium has used the therapeutic fast for excellent results in the following cases:

High blood pressure and incipient arteriosclerosis.

Disorders of the metabolic system such as arthritis, all forms of rheumatism, sciatica, and liver complaints.

Certain gastric and intestinal ailments; chronic constipation.

Chronic tonsillitis and catarrh.

All lung ailments except tuberculosis of the lungs.

Infections of kidneys and bladder.

Women's diseases.

Chronic skin diseases.

Diseases of the eye.

Periodontosis.

Nervous disorders.

Cancer, before its manifest stage (precancerosis).

Dr. Buchinger holds that the therapeutic fast is to be avoided for cases of mental imbalance, climacteric psychoses, hysteria, tuberculosis, and cancer. Cases of diphtheria or scarlet fever should be recovered for at least one year before any effort is made to fast a patient.

For further information write to Buchinger Sanatorium for Biological Therapy, Bad Pyrmont, Germany.

Dr. Shelton's Health School

The philosophy and teachings of the dean of natural hygiene, Dr. Herbert M. Shelton, have guided most American natural health practitioners for nearly 50 years.

Dr. Shelton's Health School, unique among all health clinics in the United States, is located north of San Antonio, Texas. It is primarily an educational institution. Its maxim is, "Health by healthful living."

The health school teaches how to keep fit by fasting, following by the proper use of vegetarian food, air, water, sunshine, exercise, rest and sleep, cleanliness, and emotional poise.

As a pioneer in supervised fasting therapy, Dr. Shelton, assisted by his associate, Dr. Virginia Vetrano, has treated more than 50,000 patients. For further information write, Dr. Shelton's Health School, P. O. Box 1277, San Antonio, Texas 78206.

Five Florida Health Resorts

Thousands of fortunate people have apparently found their way back to vibrant health at five Florida health resorts that base their program on Dr. Shelton's teachings.

They include Shangri-La in Bonita Springs; Orange Grove Health Ranch in Arcadia; Florida Spa in Orlando; Bay N' Gulf Home in St. Petersburg; and Esser's Hygienic Rest Ranch in Lake Worth.

The directors consider these resorts to be health schools. A health school, they will tell you, is not a hospital, clinic, or a sanatorium. It is a place where the ill may be helped back to good health; not through treatment alone, but also by learning the conditions that are necessary for the regeneration of the body's own forces of recuperation and repair.

Orange Grove Health Ranch. Five miles outside Arcadia, on a secluded, 106-acre ranch, Frank and Ann Peterson direct the Orange Grove Health Ranch. More than 2,800 fruit trees and two large organic gardens are under cultivation. One of the gardens is worked exclusively by older folks because Mr. Peterson recognizes that such socially useful activity contributes to the maintenance of good mental and physical health.

Since 1958, Mr. and Mrs. Peterson have helped hundreds

of people to overcome their health problems through fasting, raw food, fresh air, and lots of rest and relaxation. Frank Peterson once operated a successful store in Milwaukee, Wisconsin. He was forced to give it up because of crippling arthritis. Convinced that he overcame his condition by following Dr. Shelton's teachings, he decided to dedicate his life to helping other people solve their health problems.

Here are three case histories from the files at Orange Grove.

1. A 73-year-old woman whose doctor had told her that she had only a month to live. This woman had been on medication for a fluttering heart and had rebelled when told that she must spend her last month in a nursing home. Instead, she came to Orange Grove Health Ranch. When she arrived, she had to be carried out of the car. After a seven-month stay — living on raw food, oranges, and grapefruit — she had lost 48 pounds (down from 180) and normalized her heart action and blood pressure. She left the ranch looking and feeling "years younger."

2. A 77-year-old man who had suffered from arthritis for 47 years and had been diabetic for 26 years. This man's fingers were so twisted that he required help to get dressed. He was placed on a short fast, then on a raw fruit and raw vegetable regimen. Even though he stopped taking medication after 13 days, his arthritic pains subsided. Within a month he was able to pick oranges and grapefruit from the trees at the ranch. After a three-month stay he was able to leave the ranch with his arthritis and diabetes under control.

3. A 72-year-old woman with a 240 over 110 blood pressure, suffering from diabetes, arthritis, and shortness of breath. This woman was placed on a three-day fruit juice fast followed by a 30-day papaya and raw food diet — under supervision. By the end of the 30-day period, her blood pressure had returned to normal. She lost 28 pounds and was able to walk five miles daily.

Shangri-La. R. J. Cheatham, director of Shangri-La, was stricken with cancer in 1948. Medical men operated and Mr.

Cheatham decided to find out why he had become a victim of this dread disease. He studied all available material and decided that unless he changed his way of life in order to eliminate the cause of his problem, he would be affected again. He found Dr. Herbert M. Shelton's teachings and has been devoting his life to this school of living ever since. helping others to learn and to live the natural hygiene way.

Shangri-La is on 10 acres of a tropical setting in the little village of Bonita Springs, 25 miles south of Fort Myers on U.S. Highway 41. The site has about 650 fruit trees and many rare tropical plants, an excellent swimming pool, two large solaria, and boats and watercycles to use on a meandering creek that flows from the Shangri-La property all the way to the Gulf of Mexico — about four miles away.

More than 1000 people can obtain accommodations and learn a new way of life at this "Shangri-La." Fasting, improved nutrition, and corrected living habits are the primary "therapies" used for regeneration. Health lectures are scheduled five times each week. Smoking is not permitted either in the building or on the grounds.

About half the people who go to Shangri-La are interested in the supervised fasting program. The longest fast at this institution has been 84 days, with one at 80 days and another at 70 days.

Here are some cases from the Shangri-La files:

F. R. came to Shangri-La after his physician had detected an abdominal tumor the size of a grapefruit and insisted that an operation was the only solution. F. R. fasted under supervision for 31 days and recuperated for an additional three weeks. When he returned home the same physician gave him a physical examination. F. R. wrote back to the personnel at Shangri-La, "The doctor punched around all over but said that he couldn't find any sign of the tumor."

G. S. came to Shangri-La to lose weight. She was guided in a fast 84 days and then stayed on for another two months, participating in a modified dietary program, attending classes, etc., and left weighing a hundred pounds less.

O. Z. came to Shangri-La after a heart attack with blood pressure at 250 over 108. He also complained of bursitis, a spastic colon, and shooting pains in the head. His fast was for 40 days with a recuperation of three weeks. He lost 40 pounds, his blood pressure went down to 130 over 96, and he left saying he never felt better in his life.

C. H. had continuous, severe migraine headaches. After 21 days of fasting, she said, "It's like a great dark cloud has been lifted away."

H. C. had been trying all kinds of treatments for his psoriasis for 20 years but it had become progressively worse. He fasted 41 days at Shangri-La and adopted a hygienic program. Now, once again, he can wear short sleeve shirts — with no psoriasis at all.

T. J. had to be carrried up to her room when she arrived because of severe arthritis. After three weeks of fasting and two weeks recuperation, she danced a jig at a social activity the night before going home.

C. J. had become "addicted" to the enema habit but after fasting for four weeks had her first normal bowel movement in over 15 years.

H. T. came to Shangri-La with severe arthritic pain and left after only one week's fast, saying, "I now have no pain."

The food program at Shangri-La is quite strict. Here are some of their typical natural hygiene menus:

Breakfast features one or two fruits. Fruits are advised at most biological clinics — fruits such as grapefruit, oranges, loquats, strawberries, pineapples, and cherries. When melons are in season they are alternated with acid fruits.

Lunch consists of a variety of fruits such as avocados, plums, persimmons, pears, mulberries, all available varieties of grapes, apples, etc. Four different fruits are usually served at a meal. Among them are papayas, mangos, peaches, bananas, dates, dried figs, and apricots. Shangri-La does not serve bananas or sweet fruit when acid fruit is served. Mr. Cheatham feels that the avocado combines well with most foods except nuts or melons.

Dinner has a large salad as the main course. It consists of

whole lettuce leaves, whole celery stalks, whole peppers, etc., so that the complete food value is retained. All types of a available greens and nuts, usually in the shell, are served. Among them are pecans, almonds, filberts, walnuts, cashews, etc., as well as sunflower and pumpkin seeds.

Four evenings a week, cooked food is served instead of nuts. No milk, curds, cheese, eggs, fish, chicken or meat of any kind are served at Shangri-La. No salts, spices or sugar, lemon juice, or condiments, etc., are served with meals here. For those who insist on some type of dressing a powder vegetable seasoning and cold-pressed safflower seed oil is available. Desserts are taboo and between-meals snacking is discouraged.

Bay N' Gulf Hygiene Home. In 1961, Dr. J. M. Brosious moved his Hygiene Home from Pennsylvania to St. Petersburg, Florida. Dr. Brosius has a 30-year natural hygiene background. His spa is on a half-acre, 50 feet from the Gulf of Mexico. There is no industrial pollution in the Bay N' Gulf Hygiene Home environment. Using natural spring water and organic fruits and vegetables, Dr. Brosious combines fasting plus natural foods. Natural laws are the basis for helping to restore a state of harmony between one's body and Mother Nature.

Florida Spa. Thirty-five years ago, Dr. Stanley C. Weinsier, a pioneer in the field of natural healing, organized the Florida Spa in Orlando.

Located in the lake section of Orange county on a 23-acre tract, the Florida Spa has a splendid garden of organically grown vegetables as well as orange and papaya trees.

Open from October 15 to May 1 each year, the spa accommodates some 35 people and follows natural hygiene methods. It has helped countless hundreds find the path to health.

Esser's Hygienic Rest Ranch. Esser's Hygienic Rest Ranch in Lake Worth, Florida, five miles south of West Palm Beach, is ideally situated on a 10-acre tract. It can help

31 people at one time. Available to the guests are 10 professional tennis courts, and the second-largest swimming pool in Palm Beach County. Exercise, plus fasting, raw foods and vegetables, are used to hasten physical and mental rejuvenation.

Dr. William J. Esser, director of the ranch and author of *Dictionary of Foods,* uses natural hygiene methods.

All five of these Florida health schools, while operating independently of one another, serve a similar diet: two fruit meals and one vegetable meal daily.

We believe that the physical and mental health of the United States population would be greated elevated if there were 500 health schools of this type instead of so few.

Food and fasting — related therapies

Doctors should thus their patients' food revise
What is it? When the meal? And what its size?
How often? Where? Lest by some sad mistake
Ill sorted things should meet and trouble make.

Food
Is Your Best Remedy

Good nutrition is a major concern at most health spas — and especially at nature-cure clinics. Some have made nutritional therapy both an art and a science. Here are several notable examples.

The Bircher-Benner Clinic

The Bircher-Benner Clinic in Zurich, Switzerland, has led the way since 1897 in restoring health through nutritional therapy. Founded by the late Dr. Max Bircher-Benner and continued today by members of his family, this outstanding biological clinic attracts patients from all over the world.

Biological clinics evolved as a result of many advances in the science of natural healing, spearheaded by the Bircher-Benner Clinic. It deals with the whole personality, not just the physical illness of the patient — an approach widely regarded as the best and quickest way back to health.

This type of treatment is not practical for large numbers of people as in conventional mineral spring spas, since each patient must receive the individual attention of a trained practitioner for the entire day.

Dr. Bircher-Benner believed in a natural, raw-food diet which would enable the convalescent and those who have poor health to regain fitness and vitality. This form of nutrition is designed to prevent illness by increasing resistance and to help the body withstand most effectively the diseases of old age.

Dr. Bircher-Benner taught that the regular consumption of overprocessed, devitalized food contributes to impaired health. Too highly concentrated food, he believed, over-stimulates the nervous system. Interestingly, Dr. Daniel Schroeder, an American nutrition researcher, has found that there is a loss of 30 to 90 percent of nutrients as a result of freezing, processing, refining, or canning of foods.

Fresh, unspoiled food from healthy soil has unequaled health-promoting powers, according to Dr. Ralph Bircher:

"Uncooked foods have a special value as compared to heated or cooked foods. What makes the fresh apple better food than a cooked apple, or fresh, raw milk better than pasteurized or boiled milk?

"A large number of chemical properties are altered by heat and some important vitamins are lost (vitamins C and P, folic acid; and, in part, vitamin A) — vitamins that are important for the healthy functioning of endocrine glands, the mucous membrane, blood vessels, cell walls and the formation of blood."

The doctor explains: "The Bircher-Benner Clinic has found that heating destroys numerous enzymes present in the plant cells. These enzymes perform two functions that offer a further explanation of the curative effect of raw food. They produce a self-digestion of the raw food within the intestinal tract, thus relieving the digestive glands. Also, enzymes are important for the intestinal bacteria so that beneficial coli bacteria grow and drive away the pathogenic (harmful) ones. Other findings at the clinic indicate that green vegetables, especially green, leafy vegetables, benefit health to a greater extent than any other food.

Dr. Bircher declares that chlorophyl, the green coloring matter of plants, has an apparently inexhaustible fund of curative properties. "It promotes the formation of red blood cells better than iron therapy," he says. "It stimulates respiration and nitrogen metabolism of the cell tissues, improves utilization of protein, normalizes blood pressures, reduces insulin requirements, causes unpleasant body odor to disappear, heals wounds, and improves thyroid activity."

"No day without eating green leaves" is thus a major point in the guilding philosophy at the Bircher-Benner Clinic. Ruth Bircher-Benner, clinic director, will tell you that cooked foods may be added but they must be secondary in importance. "Food that has to be cooked should be only steamed," she insists, "since many of the mineral and trace elements such as iodine (larger quantities of which are necessary for the development of the intellect than for the prevention of goiter) are lost in the water in which the food has been boiled."

The clinic advocates two small meals, one at breakfast and one in the evening. The main meal is served as lunch. With this plan, snacks can be avoided. A light meal in the evening is advocated to make for better sleep.

The clinic specializes in the treatment of stomach, liver, gall bladder, intestines, kidneys, heart, and blood circulation disorders including hypertension and arteriosclerosis. The institution is a member of the Swiss Hospital Association and is officially recognized as a hospital.

Enton Hall

Auto owners take better care of their machines than they do of their own bodies, according to Dr. Robert A. Redell, eminent New Zealand osteopath and founder in 1949 of Enton Hall, Godalming, Surrey, England — just 38 miles west of London.

Amid 150 acres of parks and woodlands and enhanced by a favorable climate, Enton Hall is dedicated to renewal of health through the use of natural healing methods. We found it one of the most outstanding biological clinics we have ever seen.

We were first given a battery of tests by one of the skilled team of qualified consultants. Then a daily dietetic regimen and treatments were prescribed for us. The therapy is based on the theory that the great healer is nature itself and that the vast majority of our health problems result from ignoring natural laws.

We found that under the energetic guidance of Norman E. Jervis, managing director, each patient receives individually tailored treatment. Programs may include fasting and one or more of the following therapies: osteopathy, chiropractic adjustment, hydrotherapy, massage, colonic lavage, pyretic, sinusoidal, and ultrasonic treatments, steam cabinet treatment, and remedial exercises. In addition, there are weekly health lectures, where health questions are answered by qualified personnel.

Park-like setting Enton Hall

Enton Hall has its own herd of Ayrshires, producing milk from which yogurt is made for the 70 to 80 guests and a like number of staff members. The clinic also has its own chickens.

The paramount importance of vital foods is central to the planning of diets. Enton Hall produces much of its own food. Salad greens and vegetables are grown under ideal conditions by organic methods.

No artificial fertilizers or poisonous sprays are used. We can attest to the difference in the taste of their home-grown salads and raw vegetables.

British and Canadian artists, writers, and theatrical people — as well as members of British nobility — are frequent guests at Enton Hall. They have been coming here over the years to regain and preserve their health.

We met a young Canadian television executive who had come to Enton Hall with a serious heart condition and nervous exhaustion. When he arrived he was unable to walk without the use of two canes. After a 10-day juice fast, he reported that he felt completely renewed — physically, mentally, and spiritually. Two months after his fast and the necessary treatments he was able to walk without the use of his canes. His personal physician in Canada found that his heart and physical condition were greatly improved. When we met him, three months after his arrival, he was hard at work on a documentary film on Enton Hall itself.

Water Treatment at Enton Hall

Enton Hall uses mineral waters for numerous types of baths believed to aid in various conditions:

Natural warm mineral springs are invaluable in cases of exhaustion, in the treatment of premature aging, and in conditions where overwork has had a deteriorating effect on the body. They are also useful for underwater therapy and for the treatment of disturbances of the locomotor organs.

Pyretic baths may induce fever, increase and complete the oxidation of acid waste products in the tissues by raising body temperature and by increasing skin activity. This treatment is of the greatest value in speeding up elimination in cases of muscular rheumatism. Vapor baths and sweating blankets are also used. The treatment is both enjoyable and beneficial.

Foot baths. Two basins are filled, one with hot water and the other with cold. The patient steps in and out of each basin at one-minute intervals. This acts as a sedative and calms the nerves.

Cold water pack. Soft towels are soaked in cold water, wrung out, and applied to the body. This promotes elimination of waste material from the cells and also relieves congestion.

Wet sheet pack. First, the patient takes either a full hot bath or a hot shower. Then he is wrapped immediately in a wet sheet. A rubber sheet is placed on the wet sheet and a blanket wrapped around the rubber sheet. This prevents evaporation and loss of heat. The wet sheet is often stained with brown or yellow waste material eliminated through the skin pores.

Trunk pack. This is applied in the same manner as the wet sheet pack except that it is used only over the trunk — from under the arms to the lower portion of the hips.

Hot sitz bath. This treatment immerses the thighs and hips in warm water — often used for pelvic disorders and delayed painful menstruation.

Tyringham Naturopathic Clinic

Man has the natural right to be healthy throughout a long and happy life. Since 1967, this philosophy has guided the efforts of the staff at Tyringham Naturopathic Clinic, one of England's outstanding health establishments. Located halfway between London and Birmingham, the clinic treats more than 1,500 chronically ill patients each year, achieving great success with natural methods.

Tyringham is a nonprofit institution with relatively modest weekly charges which include lodging, food, and treatment.

This remarkable clinic occupies a 100-room Georgian mansion on attractive grounds of some 300 acres. Its director, Sidney Rose-Neil, is a qualified naturopath and osteopath.

Tyringham Clinic occupies a Georgian mansion

All who come to Tyringham — whether they have a heart condition, a weight problem, or other ailment — receive a thorough examination from a senior practioner, who also utilizes any case history supplied by the patient's own doctor. Each patient also has the benefit of any x-rays and blood tests necessary for the development of an individual program of treatment.

All of the food served at Tyringham is vegetarian and most of it is grown right on the grounds in natural compost. No chemical fertilizer is used.

The clinic treats chronic diseases of all kinds and also helps those who are simply suffering from the pressures and strains of modern life.

Among the treatments used at Tyringham are:

Dieting — vegetarian diets and fasting.

Manipulation — both osteopathic and chiropractic.

Massage — Swedish, vibro, neuromuscular, underwater.

Physiotherapy — ultraviolet and infrared radiation, ultrasonic, high vacuum, interferential, shortwave, radiant heat, traction, wax baths.

Hydrotherapy — sitz baths, Scotch douche, sauna, steam baths, packs, compresses.

Medication — homeopathic, herbal, vitamin, and mineral salt.

Balneotherapy — sulphur, brine, epsom salts, oatmeal, peat, alkaline, oxygen, and seaweed baths.

The clinic also makes use of acupuncture, relaxation, yoga, inhalation therapy, colonic irrigation, breathing exercises, and sunbathing.

Patients at Tyringham told us they had taken seaweed baths for rheumatism, pine baths for chest troubles, and oatmeal baths for skin problems.

Tyringham uses a combination of relaxation, diet, manipulation, and osteopathy for migraine sufferers, according to Director Neil.

He adds, "We have a sauna and use natural techniques like underwater massage with powerful jets for arthritics. Alternating hot- and cold-water baths stimulate the circulation and benefit some gynaecological cases. Inhaling herbal vapors and oxygen helps chest conditions and coatings of hot wax help to loosen stiff joints."

We found that while treatment occupies much of every day there is plenty of time for relaxation. Guests may choose tennis, minigolf, crouqet, swimming, sunbathing, and garden walks. Indoors there is an excellent library, a lounge, and a game room for table tennis, billiards, cards, etc. In the summer, concerts are held in the Temple of Music. Regular talks are given weekly on nutrition, acupuncture, fasting, and other subjects of interest to the guests.

Inquiries and reservations can be made at the Tyringham Naturopathic Clinic, Newport Pagnell, Bucks, England.

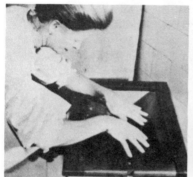 

Wax and water therapies at Tyringham

Ringberg Clinic

*Tell me what you eat
and I will tell you what you are*

— *Brillat Savarin*

Treating Cancer as a Chronic, Systemic Disease

Spa and nature-clinic methods are sometimes highly developed in the treatment of a particular ailment, often in combination with other modes of medical treatment.

Cancer is of special interest at some clinics. Perhaps the most remarkable of these institutions is the Ringberg Clinic in Tegernsee, West Germany. It is this country's oldest special hospital for internal cancer therapy — founded in 1951 by Josef Issels, doctor of medicine.

The clinic has four wards with a total of 105 beds. More than 6,000 cancer patients — 90 percent of whom have had progressive malignancy not responding to surgery, radiotherapy, or chemotherapy — have been treated at the hospital.

Therapy at the Ringberg Clinic is based on the concept that "cancer is a chronic, systemic disease" — not just a tumor alone — and requires a combined general and immunological treatment. Combined treatment includes psychotherapy, the use of autovaccines for septic foci, treatment with organ extracts to restore function, hyperpyrexia (high fever therapy), and antitumor injections. Immunotherapy is by both active immunization with mycoplasma vaccine (microorganisms intermediate between viruses and bacteria) and passive immunization from cancer cells.

Patients are treated only after they have undergone conventional surgery and irradiation and no conclusive results were claimed.

In addition to the medical director and his chief assistant there are, among others, specialists in the following fields: radiology, surgery, otolaryngology, gynecology, urology, neurology, orthopedics and ophthalmology. Five laboratory assistants, an x-ray technician, a photographer, and other technicians are involved in the diagnostic work. The 105 patients are cared for by a total of 134 full-time employees.

Because of the significance attributed today to focal poisoning with its pathogenic (disease-causing) effects in patients with cancer and other chronic disases, there is a dental ward in the clinic for the performance of scientifically founded and technically correct treatment for the removal of any oral focus of infection. This treatment is directed by an experienced specialist in oral surgery. In his area, tests for centers of infection, x-rays and, if the need arises, dental extraction are performed. Dentures are made in a dental laboratory attached to the dental ward in order to restore mastication as rapidly as possible.

In the clinic a special diet is offered, a diet developed and proven over the years to the satisfaction of clinic staff. It corresponds to modern scientific findings in the field of cancer therapy and is adapted to the disturbed metabolism of the cancer patient. The length of treatment depends on the nature, severity, and stage of the disease, as well as on the individual reaction of each patient.

Following a stay in the clinic, further treatment as an outpatient is always carried out in conjunction with the patient's family doctor.

The staff suggests visits of variable duration depending on the nature of the case.

Preventive treatment in case of increased cancer danger — four to six weeks.

Treatment prior to an operation or radiation — two to three weeks.

Treatment after operation or radiation where no tumor is present — six weeks.

Treatment of cases regarded as "incurable"; i.e., cases no longer operable or after radiation treatment for metastasis — two to three months.

The Ringberg Clinic is a private hospital operating under government license. For further information write to Dr. Josef Issels at 8133 Rottach-Egern, Am Tegernsee, West Germany.

Part III
A World Guide
To Health Spas

Meadowlark — "Friendly Hills Fellowship"

Few die of hunger
Millions die of overeating.

— *Benjamin Franklin*

Health Spas
of the United States

Arizona

Buckthorn Mineral Wells at Mesa, offers whirlpools, steam rooms, blanket packs, and massage.

Arkansas

Hot Springs National Park near Little Rock is under the supervision of the United States Government. There are 17 hot springs spas — and with many registered physicians in attendance. Treatments are given for arthritis, general injuries, and problems of the nervous system.

Holmes Sulphur Springs Baths, Sulphur Springs, has 200 acres of fertile land on which organically grown food is produced for the guests. The baths are five miles from Noel, in northwestern Arkansas. They are operated by the Philadelphia Health Foundation, a nonprofit corporation.

Free treatment may be made available to those who cannot afford to pay. Those who can pay are charged a reasonable

See also Pages 30-36.

fee. If one cannot pay, he can sometimes do light work around the grounds. For those who have no means at the moment and who cannot work, treatment may be given free with payment to be made as possible so that the funds can be applied to the needs of others in similar circumstances. Services performed include mineral water baths, wet packs, massages, colonics, and chiropractic adjustments.

California

In Napa Valley, northeast of San Francisco, there are two *Calistoga Spas*. They utilize volcanic ash mud baths, natural sulphur piped into steam cabinets, and an outdoor pool at a constant 90-degree temperature.

Palm Springs Spa utilizes natural mineral waters along with its whirlpool tubs, Scotch mist showers, salt packs, and inhalation rooms.

Twelve miles north of Palm Springs there are hundreds of hot mineral springs at *Desert Hot Springs*. There are five public mineral swimming pools. These waters were used by wandering tribes of Indians for medicinal purposes for about 1,000 years before the arrival of the settlers.

Jacumba Hot Springs, 80 miles east of San Diego, is a large center for the treatment of arthritis. Here, physical therapy is combined with soothing, hot mineral waters to get relief from this crippling condition.

Murietta Hot Springs. In October, 1797, a band of Spanish soldiers and padres of the Mission San Juan Capistrano came upon a tribe of Temecula Indians bathing in a cluster of hot springs in Southern California. The group joined the Indians in sampling the springs and found them to be relaxing and invigorating. Now, almost 200 years later, visitors from all over the world still enjoy these health-giving waters.

Located in the softly rolling foothills of Riverside county, the property was part of the vast Rancho de Temecula. In 1873, the hot springs became the property of Don Juan Murietta, thus establishing the name that has endured for more than 100 years.

Today, a 200-million-dollar building program is underway at the springs. It includes the building of eight lakes, a championship golf course, and four new swimming pools on the 300-acre ranch, as well as a health spa that occupies 15 acres.

With accommodations for more than 700 guests, Murietta Hot Springs is 85 miles south of Los Angeles. At an elevation of more than 1,300 feet it has an even, all-year climate that lends itself to overcoming tension and other health problems.

Already, thousands of health seekers have found that by combining spa facilities, which include hot mineral waters and the natural Tule mud, plus the 850-calories-per-day-menu, they are able to shed much unwanted weight. Arthritics and rheumatics have been helped by the waters.

For further information, contact Murietta Hot Springs, Murietta, California 92362.

Hidden Valley Ranch

For the past 17 years, Dr. Bernard Jensen, one of America's foremost authorities on iridology and nutrition, has led thousands of patients from all over the world to a more balanced way of life. He directs Hidden Valley Health Ranch, 1,600 feet above sea level near Escondido, California.

Dr. Jensen, lecturer and traveler, utilizes nutrition, the Father Kneipp water therapy, air, sunshine, grass, sand walks, rest, and relaxation as well as yoga to achieve his results.

The 130-acre health ranch is on a mountaintop where one can get away from the noise and tension of urban life. No freeway here — only the old stagecoach road and the pony express trail pass alongside the ranch grounds. Perhaps on a still, quiet night, one can imagine the thundering passage of yesteryear's mail riders.

Dr. Jensen's balanced daily dietary regimen, using organically grown vegetables, assures the necessary vitamins, minerals, and enzymes. He places importance in organic greens for cleansing and rebuilding the body. He maintains, "If you are green inside, you are clean inside!"

"Greens control the calcium in the body," he adds. "They are high in iron and potassium. The more bitter they are the more potassium they contain. Greens are one of the finest things for neutralizing acids in the body. The chlorophyl in greens is high in vitamin K, the antihemorrhagic vitamin. Also, there is an unusual amount of vitamins C and A in the green vegetables.

"We can absorb nutrients from greens into the digestive system faster than from any other food," the doctor says. "Less digestion is necessary for getting chlorophyl into the blood than for any of the other chemical elements. There is nothing more wonderful than greens to sweeten the body, clean the breath, and take away odors."

Dr. Jensen feels that the best daily diet should include two different fruits, at least four to six vegetables, one protein, and one starch — with fruits and vegetable juice between meals. He believes that one must consider this regimen a dietetic law.

He advocates seven simple rules for eating:

1. If not entirely comfortable in mind and body from the previous meal, one should skip the next meal.

2. Do not eat unless you have the keenest desire for the plainest food.

3. Be sure to thoroughly masticate your food.

4. Sixty percent of food eaten must be raw.

5. Your diet should be 80 percent alkaline and 20 percent acid.

6. Leave the table hungry. You can kill yourself by overeating.

7. Cook without water or high heat and with little air touching the food while cooking.

Here is Dr. Jensen's daily dietary regimen:

Before breakfast. Upon arising, one hour before breakfast, take any natural, unsweetened fruit juice. Prune, fig, apple, and black cherry juice are excellent.

Breakfast. Stewed fruit, one starch, herb tea; or two fruits, one protein, and one health drink. Creamed cottage cheese and honey are suggested if you are a heavy worker and feel that fruit alone is not enough. Eat an egg with fruit. Vary these things day by day.

Midday. A large raw salad, one starch, herb tea, and rye crisp, cornbread, or bran muffin. Raw salad vegetables include tomatoes, lettuce, watercress, celery, cucumber, grated carrots, onions, cabbage, peppers, avocado, and parsley. Starches include baked potatoes, baked banana, steamed brown rice, bread (whole wheat or rye), and cereals. Drinks may include buttermilk, raw milk, or any health drink.

Dinner. Alternate this menu with the midday meal if desired. It should consist of small raw salad, two cooked vegetables, one protein, and a broth or a health drink. Any vegetable other than potatoes may be used. Once a week use white fish and three times a week use lean meat.

For further information, rates and health lecture schedules, write to Hidden Valley Ranch, Escondido, California 92027.

Meadowlark

Meadowlark Spa, Hemet, California, a 20-acre country estate, was founded in 1957 by Evarts G. Loomis, M.D., a dedicated practitioner. This highly successful spa was the result of the vision of this man of medicine who saw from his own experience that medicine and surgery are only a small part of health therapy.

Basing his work in part on the careful, long-term research in nutrition at the Bircher-Benner Clinic in Switzerland, Dr. Loomis has been able to help patients achieve a high state of physical, mental, emotional, and spiritual health.

Dr. Loomis believes that health is much more than being free of disease; that genuine health is wholeness, the realization of one's full potential; that health is a way of life, involving our thoughts, our feelings, and our actions. "We damage ourselves as well as others," Dr. Loomis contends, "by misguided thoughts, negative emotions, and unkind acts."

A remarkable example of the results obtained by Dr. Loomis may be seen in the 72 children with brain dysfunction treated by him during the past two years. A follow-up of 63 percent of the cases indicates that 38 percent were greatly helped; 38 percent were moderately helped; and 8 percent not helped.

Dr. Loomis has been using a three-fold method of trying to reestablish homeostasis: nutrition, endocrine balance, and homeopathy.

"The results in the cases of the 72 children could have been even better," Dr. Loomis stated, "if this group had not, in many cases, already been taking a considerable amount of drugs. This definitely held back progress and interfered with the restoration of homeostasis."

In the inital survey, the children all had a careful physical examination, including a five- or six-hour glucose tolerance test, a CBC wrist x-ray for bone age, other thyroid tests, and stool analysis for evidence of carbohydrates, fat, and protein malabsorption. Most of these children were seen on referral from a neurosurgeon who had given them extensive neurological tests, including an electroencephalogram and in some cases brain biopsies.

Dr. Loomis maintains that the cornerstone of treatment for this group of children was the nutritional program: "At the beginning of the therapeutic program, especially for the severely handicapped children, I frequently put them on a diet of nothing but raw vegetables and vegetable juices and I kept them on this sometimes for two months or so before adding fruits and dairy products.

Dr. Loomis has also found that real help could be offered young people who suffer from a type of schizophrenic behavioral pattern, through the elimination of shampoos, rinses, and hair dressings that contain lead, through the elimination of excessive copper piping in homes, as well as through the use of improved diets with essential nutrients to help restore chemical balance.

Dr. Loomis called attention to a series of experiments conducted by Dr. Paul Kouchakoff of the Institute of Clinical

Chemistry, Lausanne, Switzerland, that indicated an increase of white blood corpuscles in the intestines after a meal of cooked food.

Quoting Dr. Loomis: "Dr. Kouchakoff presented several papers before the International Congress of Microbiology showing that white blood corpuscles appeared in the intestines when food was prepared at a high temperature. When an entire meal of raw food was eaten, no white blood corpuscles appeared. Dr. Kouchakoff concluded that an unhealthy situation developed internally as a result of eating cooked food that is hard to assimilate. White blood corpuscles usually appear in the intestines in the process of helping the body to fight disease."

Here are four basic characteristics of the health rejuvenation program at Meadowlark:

1. Include in your diet as high a percentage as possible of fresh raw vegetables and fruit. This should be more than 60 percent of the total intake. In cases of illness it should approach 100 percent and include fresh vegetable juices. Fresh raw seeds (sunflower, sesame, and pumpkin), nuts, wheat germ, and brewer's yeast should also be included.

Release of tension — Meadowlark

2. Avoid processed, packaged, or canned foods; especially those made of white sugar and white flour. Vegetables that require cooking (most can be eaten raw) should be cooked a minimum of time to avoid the loss of vitamins, minerals, and enzymes. Whole grain breads and cereals provide good nutrition. Avoid fried foods, preservatives, artificial sweeteners, coffee, tea, cocoa, chocolate, and all carbonated beverages. With proper nutrition, one no longer has any desire or need for stimulants. Herb teas are much more beneficial.

3. Begin each meal with a raw food such as a salad, fresh vegetable juice, or fruit. This has been found to result in the most effective digestion. The protein in fresh, green leaves and whole grains and seeds provides excellent nutrition. Much research indicates that homogenized-pasteurized milk is of lower nutritional value that either certified raw milk, buttermilk, yogurt, cottage cheese, or natural cheese. Processed cheese should be avoided.

4. Do not be discouraged if changes in health are not immediately apparent. Lasting improvement, however, is the result of patience and persistence in following the new way of living. One is often surprised by the rapidity with which changes sometimes do occur. Although nutrition is not the only factor in high-level well-being, it is the most important. Good health without good nutrition is impossible.

See the appendix for Meadowlark recipes and food hints.

For further information, rates, and reservations write to Meadowlark, 26126 Fairview Ave., Hemet, California 92343.

Vita Dell Spa

Half the population of the United States has some sort of digestive problem and 95 percent of the people of France and the United States suffer at times from constipation, according to the World Health Organization of the United Nations.

When we visited Vita Dell Spa, Desert Hot Springs, California, we found that Dr. Elva S. Acers, spa director, has helped many people overcome these conditions. Dr. Acers believes that overeating of "foodless" foods, lack of exercise, and drug poisoning are the causes of these ailments.

The director came to the natural method of healing as a result of her own experiences with drug poisoning. In 1944, she was given sulfa drugs for a strep throat. As a result of this, she believes, she suffered continuous ill health for seven years. She had internal bleeding, was unable to digest milk, and found her eyesight failing. Nothing doctors prescribed seemed to help. She was even urged to undergo surgery but she resisted and tried to help herself.

On a trial-and-error basis, Dr. Acers tried hot-and-cold sitz baths, raw carrot juice, acidophilus implantations, and vitamins. She vowed that if her health returned, she would devote the rest of her life to helping other people achieve optimum health. Slowly, she regained her health and today has evolved a system that has restored health to countless other ailing people.

Dr. Acers will tell you that people overlook the fact that it takes about four hours to empty the stomach. "You slow the process down when you eat again before you have digested the previous meal," she says. A cardinal principle is: "Don't eat unless you are hungry."

The location of Vita Dell Spa is unique. It nestles in a serene valley in the low desert, 11 miles from Palm Springs. It is in the midst of thousands of natural hot mineral springs that came into being about 1,000 B.C. when a great rupture created the San Andres Fault in California. The area is surrounded by lofty, snow-covered mountains and its pure, fresh air helps patients regain peace of mind and good health.

One of the main health aids used by Dr. Acers is the Santé Lavage system for internal cleansing. This is used to help patients overcome digestive disturbances. It is instrumented to function with and help natural persitaltic rhythms.

Dr. Acers describes a recent patient, a 45-year-old woman: 55 pounds overweight, addicted to white toast, coffee, white rice, and white flour products. She was having digestive problems and was slowly deteriorating. She was put on a three-day spring water fast, using the lavage system. In addition, Dr. Acers recommended vitamin C, exercise, and walking. She also reeducated the woman to eat properly. Within 10 weeks, the patient dropped 55 pounds and was on the road to recovery.

Another case concerned a 43-year-old beautician who, it seemed, had become poisoned as a result of the 20-year use of chemical products in her profession. She had a yellow complexion, foggy vision, her entire system was toxic, and her liver impaired. Dr. Acers used herbs, fasting, fresh fruit and vegetable juice and the lavage system. Today, after several years of natural living and having left her former work, the patient has regained her health.

A physician's wife came to Dr. Acers after a leading ophthalmologist told her that her sight was rapidly deteriorating as a result of glaucoma. Dr. Acers placed her on a therapy utilizing spleen, liver, eye, and other tissue products and megavitamin therapy. Within 10 days the glaucoma pressure was reduced and had not recurred as of this writing. Dr. Acers believes that one must treat the entire body to overcome any systemic disease.

A 44-year-old woman came to Dr. Acers after she had been told there was no hope of relieving her migraine headaches. Dr. Acers' therapy was designed to detoxify and oxygenate the patient. She recommended vitamin E, a proper diet, and lots of exercise. Within 60 days, the patient reported that the migraine headaches which had plagued her for 25 years were gone and that for the first time she was able to sleep without fear of waking up with a headache.

Vita Dell Spa has a hot mineral pool as well as individual hot mineral baths in each room. There is mineral water for drinking and nutritious organic food served buffet style.

Concerning the waters of the Desert Hot Springs area, Dr. E. A. Broue of England, an international authority on mineral waters, has said, "I have made a thorough investigation of Desert Hot Springs and have not found the like of this water anywhere else in the world. It is a pronounced curative agent."

The waters hold 11 known minerals, are crystal clear, and have provided great therapeutic help to visitors and residents through drinking and bathing. Some 150 hotels and five public spas are provided with these health-giving mineral waters. Their qualities have been recorded by 16th century Spanish mission padres, desert travelers, and generations of tribes of Cahuilla Indians.

Since accommodations are limited and prices are subject to change due to inflation, we suggest that you write to Vita Dell Spa, 13495 Palm Drive, Desert Hot Springs, California 92240.

Home of Rejuvenation

We were once staff members at Rancho La Puerta, the largest health resort in North America. One day, a guest appeared in a wheelchair. He had suffered three crippling strokes about two years previously.

The guest could move only his tongue and eyes. The rest of his body was paralyzed. He had lost most of his hair. The man who wheeled him on the grounds told us that medical men had given this unfortunate man only a short time to live. Natural health people he had consulted also held out very little hope that he would ever be able to leave his wheelchair or regain the use of his limbs.

Desperately, he had traveled all over the United States to visit doctors, health resorts, medical clinics, spiritual healers, and nature-cure people, searching for answers to his health problems — all to no avail.

But amazing things happen. Just recently we heard of the Home of Rejuvenation, a fastorium and deep-breathing center in Ramona, California, 18 miles east of Escondido. We visited the center and met its founder. He told us his story, then gave us a photograph of himself — in a wheelchair!

It was indeed Lesly Kirby, the stricken patient we had met so long before! But he was no longer confined to a wheelchair or even using crutches. Before us was a robust man, the father of a healthy six-year-old son. We found him to be a deeply religious and dedicated man who works 15 hours a day helping people regain their health.

Interestingly, the Home of Rejuvenation is one of the few health resorts we have visited where wheelchair patients are welcome. Compassion, love, and human warmth permeate the brotherly atmosphere here. Only a shortage of dedicated assistants prevents this center from becoming one of the major health centers in the United States.

Mr. Kirby told us that in 1960 he was able to leave his wheelchair and dispense with his crutches because of his many days of fasting, deep-breathing exercises, the water therapy he developed, and a deep spiritual faith that never wavered during the darkest days of his trials.

He feels that the Bible is a health book and not merely a book of religion. "If one follows the lessons that can be found in the Bible, one can gain eternal life," Mr. Kirby declares.

The Home of Rejuvenation is an unusual fastorium, located in a beautiful valley, completely surrounded by high mountains. There are organic vegetables available on the 10-acre site, plus goats and chickens.

Mr. Kirby has incorporated in his methods of rejuvenation what he believes to be the best parts of other tried and tested therapies. They include:

Massage of the lymph glands while the patient is immersed alternately in hot and cold tubs of water.

Deep-breathing exercises for about 15 minutes two or three times a day.

A one-day-a-week water fast.

A three-day water fast every 28 days.

The use of two or three enemas daily are recommended while on a water fast.

Twenty-four ounces of warm water taken daily upon arising.

Massage of lymph glands daily upon arising.

When one is fasting, Mr. Kirby strongly advocates that there be no distractions like television, radio, or the reading of newspapers.

Mr. Kirby believes that if one wants to come to the Home of Rejuvenation, he must be prepared to follow the therapy used there in order to achieve maximum results. He does not allow any smoking or alcoholic beverages or any other forms of medication.

For further information and reservations write to Lesly Kirby, Home of Rejuvenation, 1574 Wilson Road, Ramona, California 92065.

Colorado

Peaceful Meadow Health Resort near the foothills of the Rocky Mountains near Boulder has a private lake and organic vegetable gardens.

Illinois.

Spa Aliya. A new scientific concept of weight control is being utilized at Spa Aliya, Woodstock, Illinois. Anne Kopp Hyman, M.S.W., is the director.

Located 60 miles northwest of Chicago, the 150-acre spa is on a private lake with natural waterfalls. It has facilities for 30 people.

A one-week workshop for persons interested in innovative methods of weight control features international gourmet low-calorie meals and a variety of physical fitness programs including psychocalisthenics, body dynamics, yoga, dance therapy, and music and art as therapy. Resource authorities are available for work on a continuing weight-loss program for each participant.

Participants are encouraged to share their expectations of this experience, their resistance to it, their goals for themselves, and their readiness for involvement, according to Mrs. Hyman.

"The workshop leaders use tested and successful methods," she explains. "These cannot be defined or stereotyped simply as group therapy or encounter and sensitivity training techniques. The week's workshop features daily discoveries in food and drinking patterns and offers guidance in nutrition awareness."

The spa diet consists of three calorie-controlled meals daily, not to exceed 900 calories, plus a late-evening snack.

Mrs. Hyman is a former faculty member of the University of Chicago, George Williams College, and the University of Haifa School of Education.

The workshops are held monthly and some scholarships also available. For further information, write: Seminars for Continuing Education, 6312 N. Bell, Chicago, Illinois 60659.

Here are a number of other spas and health resorts in the United States on which we have not presented a detailed report but which merit consideration as places for the recovery or the maintenance of health.

Alden Mineral Springs, Alden, N.Y.; *Allison's Wells*, Way, Miss.; *Berkeley Springs*, Berkeley Springs, W. Va.; *Carlsbad Spa*, Hollywood, Fla.; *Curie Springs*, Boulder, Colo.; *Dillsboro*, Dillsboro, Ind.; *Excelsior Springs*, Excelsior Springs, Mo.; *French Lick Springs*, French Lick, Ind.; *Glenwood Springs*, Glenwood Springs, Colo.; *Harbor Island Spa*, Miami Beach, Fla.; *Hot Mineral Wells*, Niland, Calif.; *Hot Springs*, Hot Springs, Va; *Landmark Spa*, Sarasota, Fla.; *Lava Hot Springs*, Lava Hot Springs, Idaho; *Lido Spa*, Miami Beach, Fla.; *Manitou Springs*, Manitou Springs, Colo.; *Marlin*, Marlin, Texas; *Mount Clemens*, Mount Clemens, Mich.; *Olympia Hot Springs*, Olympia Hot Springs, Washington; *Palm Beach Spa*, Palm Beach, Fla.; *Safety Harbor Spa*, Safety Harbor, Fla.; *Saratoga Spa*, Saratoga Springs, N.Y.; *Sea Spa*, Hollywood, Fla.; *Sharon Spa*, Sharon, N.Y.; *Steamboat Hot Springs*, Steamboat Hot Springs, Colorado; *Sulphur*, Sulphur, Okla.; *Sun Spa*, Hollywood, Calif.; *Thermopolis*, Thermopolis, Wyo.; *Truth or Consequences*, Truth or Consequences, N.M.; *White Sulphur Springs*, White Sulphur Springs, W. Va.

We suggest that you write to the establishments in which you are interested and ask for their brochures or other information. Where only general areas are listed there may be several establishments of varying size and character. In these cases, a letter to the chamber of commerce of the city indicated may bring you helpful information.

Nature cures;
Not the physician

Health Spas of Mexico

There are some 530 designated hot mineral pools in Mexico. They have been used by the Mexican people for more than a thousand years. Montezuma and his royal court used a thermal spa in Ixtapan del Sol, about 90 miles west of Mexico City. In addition, he and his followers enjoyed some hot mineral springs right in Chapultepec park.

There are two Ixtapans: the old city, which has remained unchanged for hundreds of years; and Nuevo Ixtapan, now developed by the Mexican government as a complete health resort. Golf, deluxe American plan accommodations, horseback riding, as well as the hot mineral baths are to be found here. There are four thermal pools, two outside and two inside. This is a good example of the scores of new spas being opened all across Mexico because of an influx of health seekers from other countries.

Here is a general selection of Mexican spas — new and old — listed by states, followed by detailed descriptions of selected places of special interest:

Mexico

Atizapan, 15 miles from Mexico City; Acambay, 33 miles from Mexico City at Hacienda de Pathe; San Pedro de los Baños and La Concepción near Jocotitlan, 36 miles north of Toluca; El Chorro at Villa del Carbon; Atotonilco; Temascaltepec; Apaxco, at El Bañito, 36 miles from Mexico City; Toxhi, four miles from Temascaptepec; La Asunción at Donato Guerro and nearby El Molino.

For detailed information on this area write Dirección de Tourismo, Estado del Mexico, Toluca, Mexico, D, F., Mexico.

Morelos

Outside Cuernavaca, capital of Morelos, there are spas at Palo Bolero, Las Estacas and Tehuistla, all within a few minutes drive from the city. On Sunday these spas are crowded; we suggest packing a picnic lunch and visiting them on weekdays.

Cuautla, 62 miles from Cuernavaca via Route 115, along the base of Popacatepti and Ixtaccihuatl, is a tropical paradise.

Puebla

In the suburban area of Puebla, capital city of the state of Puebla, is an interesting spa, Agua Azul. Some 70 miles from Puebla, along Route 150, we found Tehuacan. Here are 10 hotels and mineral springs well worth visiting.

Aguas Calientes

This state, named for hot waters, has a notable lack of developed spas. There are five primitive ones. However, a new luxury spa, the Parador Zapatecas, has just opened. Write to Bienes Raines Aristos, S. A., Ave. Insurgentes sur 421, Mexico City, D. F., Mexico, for reservations and rates.

Baja California

This state is second only to the state of Mexico for spas but most are off the paved roads on primary tracks. Those out of Ensenada include the *Agua Caliente de Ramirez* (20 miles out of Ensenada on the San Felipe Road, then turn right for eight miles); the *Agua Caliente de Marconi* (22 miles south of Ensenada, then side road to Real del Castillo and eight miles beyond); *Agua Caliente de San Antonio* (27 miles *south of Ensenada, then right for nine miles); and Agua Caliente* (70 miles south to San Vicente, then left for 20 miles).

Jalisco

Outside the Jalisco state capital, Guadalajara, Lake Chapala is the favored resort area. It has several hotels, the most notable of which is Western International's *Camino Real*. West of Chapala is *San Juan Cosala* with its thermal waters.

Guanajuto

Hotel Balneario de Comanjilla is 18 miles from Leon off Route 45. German-operated, it has excellent facilities outdoors as well as rooms with private thermal baths. We met a 99-year-old Mt. Vernon, N.Y., retired tailor splashing in the pool! He had been coming to these waters for the past 35 years and told us he felt great.

San Miguel de Allende, an artist colony and handicraft center, has 13 hotels as well as rooms at the *Taboada Spa* 15 minutes from the city. In-town, the best accommodations are at *Parador San Miguel* (Artistos affiliate). Also recommended is the *Rancho El Atascadero,* with a pool, sauna, golf range, horseback riding and jumping lessons.

Michoacan

Hotel Balneario San José Purua, famed for cuisine and curative waters, has 72 rooms with private thermal baths. It is well recommended. Equally so is the American-operated *Rancho San Cayetano* at Zitacuaro, on Route 15 between Mexico City and Morelia. Thermal waters, horseback riding, and a pool are among the facilities.

Agua Blanca and rustic Zinapecuaro are best reached from Quinta Mitza, 120 miles from Mexico City and 75 miles from Morelia.

Morelia, the state's capital, has 32 hotels, of which the suburban *Villa Montaña* is internationally famous. The hotel also packs lunches for jaunts to Lake Patzcuaro or to *Spa Cointzio*.

Downtown is Western International's *Virrey de Mendoza*. Nine miles out of Morelia is *Cointzio*. It has two hot pools.

Nuevo Leon

The capital, Monterrey, has the *Topo Chico Spa*, five miles north of the city. These mineral waters help in reducing as well as in skin and rheumatic ailments. Monterrey proper has 58 hotels, many with thermal bath facilities in the rooms.

Tabasco

Although Tabasco is south of Mexico's volcanic belt line, it has 40 percent of all of Mexico's water surface. First class hotels are the *Maria Dolores*, *Olmeca*, and *Mazur*, and the *Parado Villahermosa*. There are rustic, cheap, bring-your-own-towel spas and caves at *Cocona*, *Teapa*, *Tacotaipa* and *Tapijulapa*.

Queretaro

Tequisquiapan, 12 miles from San Juan de Rio, is a basket-making center on Route 57 with four hotels containing thermal pools. There are *Las Delicias*, *Posada Tequisquiapan*, *Hotel Relax*, and *Hotel Rio* with two pools and three private thermal baths.

Mexico City

One doesn't make a spa; it happens. A volcano, minerals, some waters — and the "spa" appears with health-giving properties.

Near Mexico City's international airport, the baths have mineral parts which make it one of the world's greatest spa areas. Few outside the neighborhood of the *El Pañon de los Banos* establishment are aware that these waters have won gold medals at world expositions in Paris, Vienna, and St. Louis.

These spa waters come from the Toluca headwaters of the Larma River which feed Chapala Lake. They are both hot and cold and are chlorinated.

At *El Pañon,* one most often waits while an attendant thoroughly scrubs down the small individual pool, covers the tile floor with towels, cautions the bather about timing and leaves him to his spa pleasures.

Rio Caliente

Twelve miles north of Guadalajara, at La Primavera, a tiny Indian village in the midst of a national forest, is *Rio Caliente* (hot river), a unique nature-cure spa.

For thousands of years, Indians used the meandering, natural hot mineral river that flows through the fertile valley for curative purposes.

Rio Caliente is 4,700 feet above sea level, 200 miles from the Pacific Ocean and 350 miles below the tropic of Cancer. This combination of altitude gives the area a very favorable climate, with a mild, even temperature all year long.

The forest in and around Rio Caliente lends itself to the many legends of gold finds made there. Mexican farmers have a long-standing tradition of burying their gold in remote areas to avoid robbers.

Rio Caliente uses a papaya diet as a cleansing agent. Tropical foods served in season include chirimoya, black and white zapote, guavas, mamey, lima, jicama, malva, and guanabana. Organically grown raw greens, raw and cooked vegetables, and soups supplement the vegetarian diet.

We have found that at many of the mineral spas we have visited throughout the world, the therapeutic value of the waters is negated by an improper diet. At Rio Caliente, however, there is a synthesis of therapies. Along with the use of the large thermal mineral pool, the two private Roman baths, the natural hot mineral river, and the sauna built over the underground hot river, Rio Caliente considers nutrition the most important of all factors for health.

Yoga classes, massages, facials, nightly lectures, plus a well-rounded health program make Rio Caliente well worth visiting.

The heat of the mineral waters makes them especially beneficial for arthritis and for controlled loss of weight. The waters are alkaline, buoyant, odorless, high in iron, silicates, bicarbonates of soda, lithium, and calcium. They are low in phosphorous, salt, magnesium, and sulphur. They have a mineral taste but are not unpleasant.

Space limitations exist at Rio Caliente and we suggest that you make reservations. All inquiries should be addressed to The Spa Director, Rio Caliente, P.O. Box 1187, Guadalajara, Jalisco, Mexico.

Villa Vegetariana

David and Marlene Stry have established Villa Vegetariana as a Mexican health school on an acre and a half of lush tropical terrain three miles from the center of one of the most interesting and colorful cities in Mexico — Cuernavaca.

Basing their work on the slogan, "Man's most precious possession is good health; not gold or silver," the Stry's have utilized the favorable Mexican climate with its year-round sunshine and the many tropical fruits, to help guests achieve optimum health.

Low-cholesterol natural foods served buffet style, a swimming pool, basketball, handball, bike riding, wall tennis, yoga, hiking, Spanish classes, and organic gardening, are among the many features of this tropical paradise.

As at other spas stories of remarkable cases come naturally into the conversation.

A woman in early sixty's had spent five months in a medical hospital in traction and with all other medical modalities for the correction of arthritis. She had been considered beyond help. When she arrived at Villa Vegetariana she was in a wheelchair. Her hands were so misshapen that she was unable to comb her hair. she had to be helped in and out of her clothes. After a supervised three-week fast and two weeks on a corrective nutritional and exercise program her hands began to straighten out and she was able to walk. She left Villa Vegetariana under her own locomotion.

Another woman, close to 70, had been wearing glasses for more than 45 years. Her eyes were becoming progressively worse. At Villa Vegetariana, a nutritional program of raw fruit and vegetables was prescribed plus eye exercises based on the Bates method. After one month of treatment, the woman was able to discard her glasses.

A 48-year-old man had been suffering from psoriasis for more than 30 years. He was placed on a supervised water fast and in less than a month his skin disorder cleared up.

One does not have to be ill to enjoy the pleasures of this spa. It makes for a most interesting vacation. Dave and Marlene Stry organize interesting excursions in and around Cuernavaca and their friendliness makes one feel at home immediately. One could avoid future health problems by leading to the health lessons given there.

For further information, write to Villa Vegetariana, P.O. Box 1228, Cuernavaca, Mexico.

Rancho La Puerta

Since 1939, thousands of guests have found their way to better health at *Rancho La Puerta,* a thousand-acre health and holiday center in a peaceful valley of Baja California.

Forty miles southeast of San Diego, California — only half a mile across the United States border, Rancho La Puerta has gained a well-deserved, world-wide reputation as the largest and best-equipped health and beauty spa in North America.

Directed by Deborah S. Mazzanti, the ranch has as its slogan, "Siempre Mejor" (always better). Basing its program on an 800-calorie daily reducing diet, the ranch guarantees the overweight guest who stays on the diet the loss of at least five pounds during the first week.

The food is vegetarian — there are 40 acres of organic grapes grown on the ranch as well as other fruits and vegetables. Acidophilus milk, the herbal vapor baths, the health forums and cultural lectures, plus the Mediterranean climate, make Rancho La Puerta an outstanding place to learn how to live and thrive the natural health way.

In 1957, we were fortunate to be able to spend a year as staff members of this health paradise. One of us had been affected by overdoses of penicillin and was in very poor condition. The other had failing vision. After a one-year program including a diet of raw vegetables, the fresh air and rest, and the pleasant companionship of wonderful guests at the ranch, both of us were in the best of health and with perfect vision. Rancho La Puerta opened for us the doors to a new life of better health.

For further information, rates, and reservations, write to Rancho La Puerta, Tecate, Baja California, Mexico.

Distribution of the Hot Mineral Springs of Mexico (by States)

Aguascalientes	5	Michoacan	40
Baja California, state	11	Morelos	14
		Nayarit	17
Baja California, territory	10	Nuevo Leon	6
Campeche		Oaxaca	10
Coahuila	20	Puebla	27
Colima	10	Queretaro	17
Chiapas	11	Quintana Roo	
Chihuahua	8	San Luis Potosí	15
D. F.	14	Sinaloa	32
Durango	31	Sonora	9
Guanajuato	49	Tabasco	2
Guerrero	24	Tamaulipas	4
Hidalgo	23	Tlaxcala	7
Jalisco	32	Veracruz	11
Mexico	20	Yucatan	
		Zacatecas	10
		Total	489

Eat, drink and be merry
But tomorrow you pay

Health Spas
of Great Britain

British spas date back more than 2,000 years and today still offer relief from pain and an opportunity for restoring one's health.

Bath, in Somerset, is the oldest British spa. Its ancient Roman baths are still fed by the same unique springs. An 18th century atmosphere pervades the city, from the majestic medieval abbey to the classic squares and crescents of the Georgian bath.

All of the facilities of Bath and other British spas are available to patients referred through the British national health service plan. Today, 90 percent of the patients at Bath are from the British health service and 10 percent are private patients.

See also Pages 39-45.

Treatments include hot mud packs, hot-and-cold showers, a mineral pool, bubble bath, and sauna. About 80 outpatients are helped at Bath daily.

Royal Leamington Spa, Warwickshire, only 10 miles from Stratford-on-Avon, was founded in 1586. Its saline waters are of the muriatic-sulphate variety and their source is the remainder of a primeval sea which once covered the rock strata underlying the town. Confined for countless centuries, the waters eventually forced their way through fissures and came to the surface. They are used to treat sufferers from respiratory ailments, chronic bronchitis, asthma, and paralytic diseases.

Cheltenham Spa is in Gloucestershire, one of the loveliest towns of England, noted for its Regency terraces, its tree-lined streets and quiet gardens.

Droitwich, Britain's famous brine-center spa is in a small and attractive town whose charm derives from its fine hotels, tree-lined avenues, peaceful parks and picturesque, half-timbered houses. The spa specializes in treating rheumatic ailments. Droitwich brine is the strongest natural salt water known. It is immensely bouyant and is used in immersion baths and pools at St. Andre's Brine Baths.

Buxton, in Derbyshire, is the highest market town in England — more than 1,000 feet above sea level — in the heart of the Peak district. Its spa has been in use for more than 2,000 years. Buxton's Doric-style crescent was built in the 18th century. Its pump room still features excellent mineral waters. Thermal waters rise from the springs at a temperature of 82 degrees and are used for treatment at the Devonshire Royal Hospital.

Patients who visit Harrogate for spa treatment find excellent facilities at the *Royal Baths.* This large spa is set high up on the Pennine moors of Yorkshire's west riding.

Other British health resorts, hydros, beauty farms, and cure resorts include:

Chevin Hall Health and Beauty Hotel, Olney Yorkshire — an old stone house set on spacious grounds. The hotel specializes in weight reduction and the relief of rheumatism and arthritis.

Buxted Park Health Hydro, near Uckfield Sussex. A spa in a park of 3,000 acres where treatments include osteopathy, massage, Guss and Father Kneipp hydrotherapy, sauna, and art therapy. There are special and normal diets. It features a heated outdoor swimming pool, a beauty salon, gymnasium, and cinema.

Palm Court Renaissance Courses, Sea Front, Torquay, Devon. Housed in a comfortable seafront hotel, its treatments emphasize weight reduction, beauty and hair care, milopa facials, galvanic stimulation for muscles, and sea baths.

Kinston Clinic, Edinburgh. A Scottish baronial mansion in a 10-acre park. Treatments include hydrotherapy manipulation, massage, and corrective gymnastics. The emphasis here is on health maintenance rather than cure, with a vegetarian diet and exercise.

The Grange, Henlow, Bedfordshire. A Georgian house on spacious grounds. Treatments include Viennese physical culture, heat and foam baths, seaweed baths, massage, sauna, parafango (mud packs), wax baths. Beauty treatments include electrolysis, skin peeling, muscle toning, hand and foot waxing.

Grayshott Hall Health Centre, Grayshott, near Hindhead, Surrey. Here is a beautiful Victorian country mansion. Treatments include Japanese and soft tissue massage, colonic irrigation, sauna, Turkish bath and remedial exercise. Facilities include an indoor heated swimming pool, a beauty salon, cinema, gymnasium, golf course, and a billiard room.

Forest Mere Hydro, Liphook, Hants, occupies a Tudor mansion with a lake on the grounds. It is registered as a nursing home with special facilities for people needing medical supervision, either for dieting or for convalescence. Treatments include massage, sauna, steam bath, and remedial exercise. This hydro also features physiotherapy, a heated outdoor swimming pool, sailing, golf, and riding.

Thirlmere Nature-cure Hydro, Bexhill-on-Sea, Sussex. A very quiet, small seaside hotel where treatments are based on nature-cure with massage and heat baths.

Summerfields-near-Tumbridge Wells, Kent, specializing in the early control of biological aging. Treatments include sauna and massage. There is an indoor heated swimming pool.

Champneys in the Chiltern Hills

Champneys, established in 1925, is an outstanding nature-cure resort. Founded by the late Stanley Lief, it is at present under the direction of his son Peter Lief.

One hundred guests are accommodated at Champneys in a country mansion, located in the Chiltern Hills of Herfordshire. Guests are taught the nature-cure philosophy and they often experience the eradication of disease.

Director Lief believes that rest, relaxation, and exercise are the basic essentials of all therapies leading to the elimination of poisonous matter from the body.

"The unorthodox revolutionary methods of approach employed at Champneys Nature-cure Resort recognize and deal with health problems," according to Mr. Lief. "They have made this centre of natural healing the 'Mecca of the uncured.' The nature-cure treatments administered are based on the discovery and removal of causes rather than the treatment of the effects of disease."

Shrub Land Hall Health Clinic, near Ipswich, Suffolk. A Georgian house with spacious gardens. Treatments, under medical supervision, include chiropractic manipulation, colonic irrigation, Guss and Kneipp hydrotherapy, and soft tissue massage. There is a vegetarian diet, a heated outdoor swimming pool, croquet, putting, and a gymnasium.

Mineral waters and inhalation, Mont-Dore

Give me a good digestion, Lord
and also something to digest;
Give me a healthy body, Lord
With sense to keep it at its best.

Health Spas
of France

Vichy

France has 1,200 mineral springs. The sodium bicarbonate waters of Vichy occupy first place because of their unusual qualities. These waters are for drinking and bathing. They are reputed to have a profound generalized action on metabolism and digestion.

Recent research on the ionic exchange between the interstitial tissues and alkaline water absorbed through the skin have made it possible to show how hydrotherapy hastens the cure.

Three different types of showers are used at Vichy: upright, recumbent, and the "Vichy shower" in which two attendants (facing each other) give a vigorous massage while spraying a continous shower over the entire body of the reclining patient.

There are two types of massage: dry massage and

pneumatic massage with an apparatus which utilizes cupping and acts more deeply than a dry massage.

There are three types of douches: intestinal, rectal, and vaginal.

Mineral baths include underwater showers, carbon dioxide and alternate hot-and-cold foot baths. In addition, use is made of mud and sauna baths, inhalations, remedial gymnastics, electroradiology, and dietetics.

The Vichy cure seems to be effective in problems of digestion due to faulty nutrition. The cure includes the taking of waters from natural springs; the specific spring, dosage, and frequency prescribed by the consultant in charge.

Each cure is individual and is constantly adapted to the reaction of the patient. Patients have at their disposal all the resources of balneotherapy, hydrotherapy, fangotherapy (mud packs), mechanotherapy, thermotherapy, and electroradiology.

The Vichy cure seems also to have a deep and lasting effect in liver complaints, allergies of an alimentary and digestive nature, as well as in diabetes, gout, and gallstones.

Aix-les-Bains, in the heart of the French Alps is a national thermal establishment under state management (ministry of health). It is world renowned for the treatment of all kinds of rheumatic complaints, neuralgia, aftereffects of fractures and wounds, and infantile paralysis.

There are two distinct springs at the establishment: sulphurous calcic and radioactive, both emerging from a single underground current. There are various types of douches; and spray, rain, circle, spinal, and sitz baths. They are given at various temperatures as needed. In addition, the natural mineral waters are part of the drinking cure.

More than 150 specialists in douche and massage trained at a school attached to the Lyon Faculty of Medicine are in attendance at the Aix-les-Bains.

Mont-Dore is one of the most ancient spas in France. Excavations have revealed important remains of Roman baths and even installations dating from the time of the Gauls.

It was not until the 19th century than an establishment was built worthy of the therapeutic results obtained from Mont-Dore water in the treatment of respiratory ailments. In the past 30 years, modernization has made it one of the finest spas in Europe.

Thalassotherapy centers. Using the curative qualities of sea water and marine climate for therapeutic purposes is the definition of thalassotherapy, a word deriving from the Greek root *thalassa,* the sea; and *therapeia,* treatment.

France has more than 1,800 miles of coastline and 10 thalassotherapy centers. Four are on the coast facing the

Thalassotherapy — rejuvenation by the sea

English Channel; two on the Atlantic Ocean; and four on the Mediterranean Sea.

The salt water and sea air health centers on the French coast employ bathing techniques based on those in use at certain hot springs healing centers throughout the world. Sea water, the richest of natural waters, is heated to the desired temperatures. The patient may also be given mud baths and baths containing seaweed, a plant with many valuable health-restoring properties. Sea water contains such elements as sodium, magnesium, calcium, potassium, iodine, etc., and oligo elements whose presence catalyzes the vital reaction.

Using the latest techniques in hydrotherapy, the 10 centers treat rheumatism, painful disorders of the spinal column, overwork, and depressive conditions.

Each health center specializes in selected treatments which depend on the regional climate and time of the year. They are conducted by specially trained technical and medical personnel who also do continuous research in this new field of therapeutic medicine.

Gold that buys health
Can never be ill spent

— Webster

Health Spas
of East Germany

There are now six health resorts available to foreign visitors in the German Democratic Republic. The guests stay in modern, furnished sanatoria and receive individual treatment from experienced specialists and trained technical personnel. All resorts are equipped with the diagnostic and therapeutic installations needed for a beneficial cure.

Bad Elster State Spa. This spa is in a small town deep in a valley between the densely wooded hills of the Ore mountains, about 10 miles from the border of Czechoslovakia. The mild climate seems to stimulate metabolic processes.

The spa boasts 16 mineral springs and has a house for mud bathing on the banks of the White Elster River. It treats inflammation of the kidneys, rheumatism, diseases of the motor system, metabolic illnesses, chronic heart and blood vessel complaints, liver and gall bladder troubles, blood diseases, gynecological problems, and nervous ailments. More than 25,000 guests are helped annually. There are three sanatoria reserved for foreigners.

Bad Brambach is located only 10 miles south of Bad Elster but at an elevation of 1,800 feet. This spa has typical, stimulating subalpine climate. Wooded hills protect it from harsh winds. Pure air and radioactive atmosphere and waters help in the healing process, according to doctors at the spa. Since there is no fog or mist, Brambach has become a favorite spa for gout and rheumatism. More than 10,000 patients are helped here annually.

There are more than 20 differing medical mineral fountains in Bad Brambach for drinking, bathing, and mud baths. One of them is the strongest radium fountain in the world containing valuable minerals and free carbonic acid.

Bad Liebenstein Heart Spa is 1,200 feet above sea level on the southwest slope of the Thuringian Forest. There is an excellent park outside the spa with beech and pine woods. Liebenstein treats nervous complaints and circulatory problems.

Berggiesshubel Kneipp Bath Spa. This spa, 1,000 feet above sea level in the Gottleuba valley, treats the following ailments: diseases of the motor system, chronic heart and blood vessel complaints, stomach and intestinal ailments, gland diseases, diabetes, and nervous exhaustion.

Potsdam Neufahrland Diet Sanatorium specializes in alimentary therapeutics. It is near sea level in the Mecklenburg lake district. Here are treated stomach, intestinal, liver, and gall bladder complaints as well as skin diseases and diseases of the kidney and urinary passages.

Heiligendamm Sanatorium, a Baltic Sea health resort, is the oldest German seaside resort, It is surrounded by beech woods in a coastal climate. Diseases of the motor system, metabolic problems, stomach and intestinal disorders, diseases of the respiratory system, skin diseases, and nervous exhaustion are treated here.

All of the spas of East Germany have salt water springs for bathing and physical therapy and special diets that are prescribed by the spa physicians. A stay of a minimum of 21 days is required to fortify and accelerate the body's entire defense.

Further bookings and travel information and rates can be obtained directly from the German Travel Office, Berlin N 5, Friedrichstrasse 110-112, German Democratic Republic.

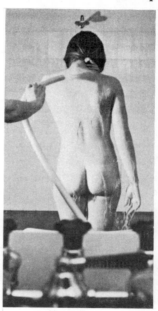

Mineral waters under pressure

Climate and scenery aid in "the cure"

Things sweet to taste
prove in digestion sour

— **Shakespeare**

Health Spas
of West Germany

West Germany has more than 240 mineral, mud, marine, Kneipp, and climatic health resorts. Of this number, 108 are state-operated. There is a spa for almost every ailment.

Both German and foreign patients with arthritis and diseases of the joints can be helped at 64 of these spas. Asthma is treated at 11. Thirty-one spas relieve catarrhs of the respiratory tract. Nature-cure methods are utilized in the treatments at all these resorts.

Rheumatic complaints are alleviated at *Bad Nauheim* spa, 30 miles north of Frankfurt. Heart and circulatory problems as well as blood pressure disorders are treated here.

The spa springs are rich in carbonic acid. The water from each spring can be used in a variety of different forms and

See also Pages 27-30 and 47-49.

mixtures. Each patient at Bad Nauheim gets a special prescription from the doctor for the type of mineral baths best suited to his ailment.

Present research at Bad Nauheim is conducted at the Kerckhoff Cardiac Research Institute of the Max Planck Society. "Research in order to help," is the motto of Arthur Weber, M. D., who established a foundation in Bad Nauheim for the promotion of scientific work on problems of the coronary blood vessels. Scientists have found that Bad Nauheim baths dilate these blood vessels, reduce the work of the heart, and improve the blood supply of the circulatory system. The springs also help rheumatic diseases because they mobilize the healing powers of the body, alleviate rheumatic pain, relax the muscles, and improve the mobility of the joints.

Scientific institutes aid in spa therapy

Individual diet is an important part of the spa therapy and is prescribed for each patient by the attending doctor.

Medical doctors at German spas believe that hydrotherapy is far superior to the so-called wonder drugs in helping arthritics. Research reported at European and international congresses outline the serious side effects of the cortisones that can outweigh their positive values.

Hydrotherapy has helped arthritics for thousands of years. German spas like *Baden-Baden* — perhaps the most famous of all spas, *Aix-la Chapelle*, and *Wiesbaden*, have been greatly valued for the healing properties of their waters for more

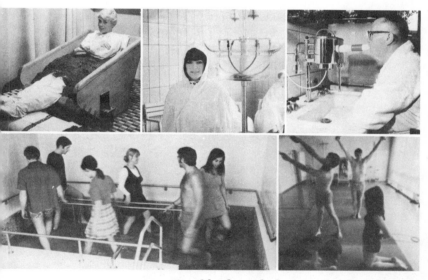

Sand baths, inhalation, physical therapy

than 2,000 years. Brine water, sulphur springs, mud and peat baths are used. Resorts for arthritics located on the fringe of high mountains combine climatic benefits with the advantage of balneotherapy (baths). The use of this therapy apparently leads to a basic readjustment of the nervous system.

Ailments treated successfully at resorts for arthritic sufferers include: primary chronic articular rheumatism, rheumatic inflammation of the spinal column, and maladjustment of the spinal column.

If hydrotherapy is begun early enough, it seems, recovery from a rheumatic ailment is possible. In cases where the joints and spinal column can no longer be influenced anatomically, the patient can nevertheless be freed from pain and improved functioning of the joints can be achieved.

Further information and brochures can be obtained at the German National Tourist Offices at 61 Conduit Street, London, W. I., England; 500 Fifth Avenue, New York City, N.Y. 10036; 323 Geary Street, San Francisco, California 94102; or at 11 South La Salle Street, Chicago, Illinois 60603.

Underwater massage, thermal baths

Health Spas
of the Soviet Union

A choice of more than 3,500 spas are now available to the health seeker who comes to the Soviet Union.

After the 1917 revolution, there were only 36 spas and resorts all of which had been started in the 18th century by Peter the Great. He had experienced the healing power of mineral waters in Germany and France. Before the revolution, Russian aristocrats traveled to Baden-Baden, Carlsbad, and Vichy.

Lenin, father of the Russian revolution, increased the number of Russian spas to 500. Today more than 19 million people annually utilize more than 4,500 spas and mineral and thermal springs and are helped to better health.

In the Soviet Union, spas are called Kur-Orte. They are placed where patients take treatments for specific

Relaxing thermal bathing

ailments and are of four types: forest, mountain, prairie, and seaside.

A major Soviet innovation is the idea of floating sanatoria and rest homes on board comfortable ships completely equipped for all types of therapy. These ships sail along the Volga, the Oka, and other large rivers from June through September. One such ship sails from Moscow to Astrakhan and back in 24 days. It has facilities for hydrotherapy and physiotherapy — plus libraries, a cinema, game rooms, mineral pools, and cultural events. The ship stops at Gorki; Ulyanovsk, birthplace of Lenin; Saratov; Kuibyshev; and Volgograd, site of the Battle of Stalingrad, to allow passengers to go on sightseeing tours.

For Soviet workers there are night-and-day sanatoria attached to factories and some 5,000 reconditioning centers where all types of health ailments are treated with exercise, proper nutrition, and all natural healing methods, In Moscow is the Academy of Nutrition where the latest health ideas are studied by scientists from all over the country. An intensive national campaign to discourage alcoholism and smoking is now being conducted by the Academy.

Odessa is the center of large cultural and scientific establishments, including the Research Institute of Health Resort Therapy and Physiotherapy. Here, during the past few years, they have found that the medicinal mud contains folliculin, stilbestrol, chlorophyl, carotene, and various trace elements.

Odessa is a seaside resort, ideal for both recuperation and for an enjoyable holiday. Summers are hot, ideal for ocean bathing. Autumn is warm and the winters are mild with light frost.

Thirteen mineral springs for drinking and bathing and many sanatoria are to be found in the area. They treat circulatory diseases, functional and organic nervous disorders, locomotory problems as well as tubercular, urological, and gynecological diseases.

Kislovodsk, north of Tiflis, is the oldest and most famous mineral water center of old Russia. This conglomeration of spas is embedded in the foothills of the northern Caucasus and has more than 130 mineral springs. The area has more than 300 sunny days free of fog, and the winters are mild. The spa was founded by Peter the Great in 1717. It features narzan for drinking in its 25 sanatoria. Narzan contains small amounts of silver, copper, iron, manganese, iodine, and bromine, in a hydrocarbonate-sulphate-alkali mineral water.

Discovered in 1810, *Zheleznovodsk,* has long treated ulcers and liver troubles, Its popularity for more than 160 years is due, in great part, to the 22 mineral springs which feature hot calcium waters. There is a great similarity between this spa and Karlovy Vary (Carlsbad), Czechoslovakia, according to Soviet spa authorities.

All of these great spa centers effectively use climato-therapy, thalassotherapy (sea waters), sun and air baths, as well as sleep therapy.

The physiotherapeutic facilities make it possible in Soviet spas to use all modern forms of electrotherapy, phototherapy, terrain walks, remedial gymnastics, oxygen therapy, as well as inhalatoria, and open-air sleeping pavillions. The mineral waters include sodium, hydrocarbonate, sulphate, and calcium groups. For each spa and for each mineral spring, therapy for a specific disease is determined by the central institute.

Yalta, Sochi, and Kislovodsk — each has a basic sana-torium as an experimental station for all the other resorts in the area. At these centers, therapeutic methods are established including diets, sports, and cultural activities.

Northern Siberia as well as Kazakhatan, with an all-year sunny season, have spas. The center of this spa area is around the Black Sea. More than a million Soviet and foreign guests are treated in this area.

Five of the best-known centers in the Black Sea area include Yalta, Odessa, Sochi, Kislovodsk and Zheleznovdsk. (The Livadi Palace, meeting place of the Big Three at the Yalta Conference, is now used as a spa for heart patients.)

Open-air rest therapy at Sochi

Yalta is built in the form of an amphitheatre, sloping down the shores of a deep bay surrounded by mountains. To the north, the city is shielded by dense forests, making for a warm, Mediterranean climate. There are beautiful parks, vineyards, and palaces. The sunshine, mild climate, and quiet seas make Yalta one of the best spas for the treatment of lung diseases and functional disorders. There are 23 well-equipped sanatoria and modern diagnostic and physiotherapeutic facilities. Yalta also houses the Sechenov Research Institute of Medical Climatology and Climatotherapy that constantly evaluates the effectiveness of various therapies. In all the Yalta sanatoria, respiratory, cardiovascular, and nervous diseases are treated.

The beach of *Sochi-Matsesta* which extends for 65 miles, hosts more than 18,000 guests in the sanatoria that surround the city. The climate is humid, subtropical with perennial vegetation, and is sheltered by the western hills of the Caucasus. Spa facilities consist mainly of the medicinal wells of Matsesta, where there are very effective sulphur springs. Here, there is prophylactic treatment for cardiovascular, locomotor, dermatological, and gynecological diseases. Sulphur, iodine, boric acid, and nitrogen are in the spa waters. Sochi gets winter rain but hardly any snow.

The Russian spa physician, as all other Soviet medical

personnel, has to take postgraduate courses every five years for at least six months.

Every spa doctor has only three new patients a day, and an average sanatorium has about 50 physicians.

There is a diet physician for every four sanatoria. The patient typically has a choice of five menus. Once a week they practice a type of fast, which is called an "unloading day." The Soviet spas utilize the day to help patients lose extra weight. Using five different types of diet, spa specialists let patients dine six times daily: at 8 a.m., 11 a.m., 2 p.m., 4 p.m., 7 and 9 p.m.

Five types of diet used on "unloading days" are:

Fruit-cooked rice day (two ounces of cooked rice, two pounds of fruit in season).

Fruit-meat day (five ounces of lean meat, two pounds of fruit in season).

Milk day (six glasses of raw skim milk).

Fruit-vegetable day (three pounds of fruit and assorted vegetables together).

Fruit day (three pounds of apples, pears, or low-calorie fruit in season).

Soviet spa specialists, drawing on the teachings of Pavlov, consider sleep a health habit of great importance. Pavlov held that normal sleep rests the nervous centers and brain and that normal sleep can be developed in the average man or woman by training the brain to develop an appropriate conditioned reflex.

Here are some Soviet spa recommendations for training the brain to sleep:

Walk for at least half an hour before retiring.

Have plenty of fresh air in your bedroom.

Air your bedroom while you are out walking.

Take alternating hot-and-cold foot baths for about five minutes before retiring.

No food of any kind for several hours before retiring.

No drinks of any kind, including warm ones, before retiring.

One should sleep alone.

No bed clothing that puts pressure on any part of the body.

Sleep either flat on your back or on your right side. Sleeping on the left side, it is believed, hinders the working of the heart and other organs.

Soviet cures at the night sanatorium are of major interest. How many employees all over the world go on working despite health problems because they cannot afford to take time off for treatment? In most cases they take pills and try the well-intentioned health advice of friends and go on working — if they can.

When a Soviet worker suffers a health problem due to his job, he can be treated without having to take time off from his work.

The Soviet worker sees his doctor, a union member, who may suggest that he take an "all-night cure." At quitting time, the worker goes to a night sanatorium, usually located in a nearby park or forest. He stays there overnight while treatment is administered, and goes back to the job in the morning.

Workers can take three sets of treatment per year, each consisting of 22 treatments, either day or night, depending

Semashko Mud Cure Center

on the shift they work. Treatments include exactly prescribed food, recreation, exercise, and sleep. Soviet doctors, unlike ours, do not depend so much on drugs because they tend to prefer safer, tested, natural methods. For example, for the treatment of arthritis and associated problems, they often use sea water baths, mud baths, ultrasonic therapy, and massage.

Bursitis, treated once a year in a night sanatorium, can be fully controlled. For recuperation after an operation or the flu, full recovery is usually achieved without the chronic aftereffects many of us experience.

There are more than 1,900 round-the-clock treatment facilities associated with Russian factories, all staffed by doctors, nurses, and technicians. The main objective is prevention, helping workers to avoid developing industrial ailments; and, of course, this service greatly reduces absenteeism. In addition, the centers treat many chronic ailments such as poor digestion, constipation, and colds.

The highest price a patient may be charged is 16 rubles, or about $17, for 24 nights — about 75 cents per night. The average Soviet worker actually pays only about half that much since the charge is fixed by his trade union based on wages, dependents, etc.

People take these cures who wouldn't if they had to quit work to go to one of the many spas throughout the Soviet Union.

In addition to the many regular and specialized hospitals in Russia, located in various districts, the largest factories also have their own general hospitals. There are about 1,500 such medical centers in the Soviet Union with almost 200,000 beds.

Specialists and doctors working in these hospitals continually tour the factories. They practice preventive medicine and have regular open office hours in the plants every day.

One can make reservations at Russian spas either through his own travel agent or directly with Intourist. In the United States: 44 E. 49th Street, New York City, N.Y. 10017. There is an off-season discount rate from October through April.

With health, everything is a source of pleasure
— *Schopenhauer*

Health Spas of Czechoslovakia

Czechoslovakia, home of 52 mineral water health spas and more than 1,900 springs of curative waters, plays host annually to more than 350,000 Czech and foreign guests, seeking either to preserve or regain their health.

All Czech spas have specialized sanatoria for a specific group of diseases. There are special establishments for foreign patients. In all the spas there is constant medical and nursing service, In addition, there are outpatient spa institutes.

Taking the mineral water seems to rejuvenate the person who wants to do something for his health; and for the healthy, it seems to aid in preventing illness.

Every year about 220,000 Czech workers and members of their families are granted free spa treatment for three weeks. Train fare and expenses are paid by the national health insurance service.

Foreign guests pay a fixed, daily, all-inclusive rate. This is a very low price which covers all therapeutic procedures, doctors' visits, accommodations, and nutrition, according to the principles of modern dietetics.

Mineral waters are used for baths, drinking, or inhalation as vapor. Occasionally, they are also employed for the irrigation of various body cavities. Catarrhal respiratory diseases and their aftereffects such as asthma are treated with alkaline or plain saline waters. Cardiac patients are treated with carbonic acid baths.

Artereosclerosis and hyperthyroidism are treated with waters containing iodine. Changes associated with old age are believed to be beneficially influenced via the gonads by the use of metallic thermal waters; and, especially in women, by peat baths.

Sulphur baths have an effect on skin conditions. Alkaline, sodium chloride or sulphate waters are used in restoring the disturbed diabetic and gout metabolism to normal. Women's endocrine diseases such as sterility, are apparently helped by peat baths together with chalybeate (iron salts) and carbonated waters.

In inflammatory gynecological conditions, hyperthermal and brine baths are also used. For gastric diseases alkaline waters are used, whereas a deficiency of hydrochloric acid and digestive ferments can be treated with acidulous, saline waters.

A content of sodium or magnesium sulphate exerts a favorable influence on constipation.

Obesity is also treated at all Czech spas. Spa treatment not only reduces the patient's weight, but also treats accompanying diseases of the heart, joints, respiratory organs, skin, urethra, as well as functional and organic nervous diseases.

Carlsbad, once the health playground of nobility and the aristocrats of Europe, today finds the visitor most probably a factory worker from West Germany, Leningrad, or Prague. With its inclusion in modern Czechoslovakia its name is now Karlovy Vary.

The history of Carlsbad began in 1358, when Charles IV,

then the Holy Roman Emperor and King of Bohemia, built a hunting lodge near the hot mineral springs. In the more than 600 years since, it has aided millions of people in finding health through its healing waters. Numerous memorial plaques throughout the cities attest to this, expressing gratitude in both prose and poetry.

Sultans, millionaires, writers, artists, and nobility have all their day in the mineral waters. Franz Josef, Austrian emperor, had a special bath built for his use in 1805. He made five visits to the mineral springs.

Today, more than 50,000 guests suffering from digestive, liver, and metabolic diseases, as well as obesity are helped annually at this world-famous spa. Carlsbad, with 40 differing hot mineral springs, has one renowned spring, Vridlo, rising from a depth of more than 5,000 feet. Its waters shoot up to a height of 36 feet. It produces some two million liters of medicinal waters daily at a temperature of 161 degrees (72 degrees centigrade).

Most visitors to Carlsbad — it is hard to remember that it is now Karlovy Vary — enroll for treatment in one of its sanatoria, where they spend an average of 21 to 28 days. The guests may be seen with their ever-present china cups from which they sip the mineral waters as prescribed by the doctor assigned to them. This is the drinking cure which brings people here. Walking and drinking the waters three times a day is a very important ritual.

Dr. Leo Hruby, spa director, says that this is only natural. "Americans often don't understand the real nature and essence of a spa. It is not a place where one goes for gambling or nightclubs or even to play golf. One comes here to be rejuvenated."

The doctor is totally dedicated to the central premise of spa therapy: mineral-rich water acts on the body in a way that corrects chemical imbalances and promotes healing.

Marianske Lazne (Marienbad) is a spa where we recently took a four week "cure." Our treatments started with a thorough medical examination by a doctor assigned to us.

She followed our progress, week by week, and was available for consultation at all times.

Based on the medical examination, a plan of treatment and diet was outlined for us. Our hydrotherapy consisted of radon and carbon dioxide baths, swimming in warm mineral water pools, sauna, remedial gymnastics, steam inhalation, dental work, and the "drinking cure" of mineral waters.

Marianske Lazne at Marienbad

There are 39 mineral springs in Marienbad, and the doctor assigned us to three specific springs. We drank a one-fourth liter glass of mineral water from each spring before every meal. This was an important part of the cure therapy. A special dining room was assigned for our meals.

We were able to call on our doctor for any additional medical therapy we felt we needed, and at no additional cost. My wife was helped with dental work and gynecological treatment.

With each regular weekly check-up, new medical treatments were prescribed if the doctor thought them necessary. We frequently had as many as five treatments in one day. Our afternoons were usually free for rest and recreation.

Evenings were occupied with cultural events such as concerts, movies, dances, or German and Czech television programs.

One of the interesting therapies recommended was the "terrain cure." A network of footpaths has been laid out through the woods adjoining the spa parks. Trees are marked to indicate specific trails for patients with particular health problems. These trails are mapped out according to how flat, how steep, shade or sun, proper distance, etc.

At the end of our cure period, there was a final medical report, with recommendations for further home treatment addressed to our home physician.

Needless to say, we were much impressed with the warmth and friendliness of the entire spa staff, as well as the amazingly low price for our four-week stay.

The spa is available for treatments or vacations, all year long. For further information, rates and reservations, address: The Director, Marianske Lazne Spa, Marianske Lazne, Czechoslovakia.

Some other outstanding Czechoslovakian health spas are:

Bardejov was founded in the 13th century. Located amid pine forests, its 17 mineral springs have various chemical compositions and contain large amounts of carbon dioxide. Here are treated diseases of the digestive system and defects of diabetes and obesity as well as diseases of the respiratory tract.

Bojnice was already in use in the 12th century. It became a town in 1244. It has six thermal springs, thermal mud, four bathing pools, and a bath center. Here are treated nervous diseases and those of the motor system. For the tourist there is a thermal swimming pool, and an interesting and well-stocked zoo.

Brusno was already known in the 15th century. Situated in pine forests, it has alkaline sulphur mineral springs which offer help for diseases of the liver, gall bladder, and pancreas.

Cjz, with an abundance of sunshine and mineral waters rich in iodine, is a spa founded in the 13th century. Here for more than 600 years patients have been treated for arteriosclerosis, chronic inflammation of the bones, and diseases of the motor system.

Dudince was registered in the 18th century as a bath spa, with mineral waters containing a great amount of carbon dioxide and sulphur. There is a large thermal swimming pool and outdoor camping sites. A great deal of success is experienced in treating nervous diseases and ailments of the motor system.

Novy Smokovec is a spa with a stimulating climate and the beauties of pine forests and much sunshine. It is a center of winter sports. Here one sees excellent results achieved for patients with problems of the respiratory tract, neuroses, and states of mental and physical exhaustion.

Korytnica, a most interesting spa in needle-leaf forests, has six mineral springs belonging to the group of the most healthful waters. Here patients find relief for diseases of the stomach, duodenal ulcers, liver problems, and diabetes. There are drinking cures, water cures, and peat compresses.

Kovacova has hot mineral water swimming pools. Located in a pine tree forest, it offers help to patients with nervous diseases and problems of locomotion.

Jachymov, an outstanding Czech spa, treats gout and other diseases of the joints, the muscles, and the circulatory system.

Jesenik (Graefenberg) treats unspecific diseases of the respiratory tract.

Luhacovice treats diseases of the digestive tract and diabetes mellitus as well as unspecific respiratory diseases.

Lucky is located in the beautiful climatic region of the High Tatras. The alkaline mineral water baths contain carbon dioxide and calcium. Women's diseases are treated with peat compresses and a thermal swimming pool.

Nimnica, the newest Czech spa, has alkaline mineral waters which neutralize stomach acids. Its treatments have also been found to be outstanding by patients suffering from respiratory diseases.

Piestany is a world-renowned spa which had already achieved fame in the 12th century for treatment of rheumatism, arthritis, and diseases of the nervous system. It enjoys a unique climate for the growth of tropical plants. Its thermal waters contain sulphurous compounds including hydrogen sulphide.

Rajecke Teplice is known for its heat compresses and thermal waters which are used to treat diseases of locomotion, nervous exhaustion from overwork, arteriosclerosis, and depression.

Sliac is a spa in use since the 13th century. It has five mineral springs with remarkably isothermic waters (constant temperature) of value in treating circulatory system disorders — heart, blood pressure, arteriosclerosis, Burger's disease, and thrombosis.

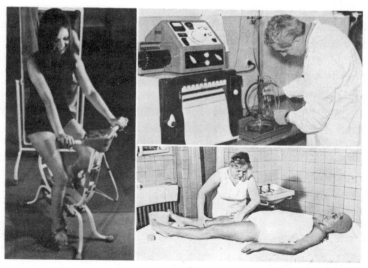

Science and skill, physical therapy

Sklene Teplice has been operating continuously since the 18th century. Its thermal waters help in women's diseases as well as problems of locomotion.

Smrdaky has been helping sufferers with skin problems and locomotion since the 15th century. Its mineral waters have the highest concentration of sulphur in central Europe.

Strbske Pleso, because of its high altitude, is the outstanding spa in Czechoslovakia for treatment of asthma, allergic colds, and other respiratory diseases.

Trencianske Teplice was already in use in the second century. In the 16th century it became famous as the spa used by Hungarian nobility. Its thermal waters contain alkaline and sulphurous elements. Its waters are used in treating patients suffering from inflammations of the leg veins, chronic inflammation of the respiratory tract, and diseases of the motor system.

Turcianske Teplice has been helping patients since 1281. Its mineral waters are used for kidney and urinary ailments.

Vysne Ruzbachy, a 14th century spa in a charming valley, has mineral waters containing a high concentration of carbon dioxide. Patients with high and low blood pressure and nervous disorders find relief in the thermal swimming pools and the curative springs.

In addition to the institutes for treatment of adult patients, some Czech spas are devoted exclusively to the treatment of adolescents and children.

Czech spas are open year-round. The main season is July through August. Rates drop substantially from October to mid-May. For additional information and particulars concerning spa treatment, apply to the management of the respective spa or to Balnea, Prague 1, Parizska 11, or to your travel agent.

Health Spas
of Austria

There are 94 health spas, climatic resorts, mineral water springs, and Father Kneipp centers in Austria. Among them: the natural hot air "emanatorium" in the underground thermal gallery at Bad Gastein-Boeckstein in the Salzburg province; and Bad Hall in upper Austria, specializing in ocular spray treatment. There is also an open-air "therapy garden" at Bad Schallerbach and many underwater therapy pools and indoor swimming pools with thermal waters.

Some spas are located at low altitudes, others in the hilly country of the Alpine forest lands; still others high up in the Alpine valleys. Many Austrian spas are away from main roads. Bad Gleichenberg is closed to motor traffic altogether.

The Salzburg Therapeutic Center has available in its vicinity more than 10,000 beds for the use of outpatients. The center is operated by the city of Salzburg with medical

Physical therapy in tranquil surroundings

treatment supervised by the Institute for Balneotherapy Research, under the direction of Professor Inama. Approved and tested methods used in spas all over the world are also utilized here. This spa operates all through the year.

Treatments used at various Austrian spas include:

Individual baths with thermal, sulphur, iodine, radon, bitumen and peat waters; also natural carbonic acid baths, carbonic acid gas baths, peat and mud baths, and natural steam baths.

Underwater gymnastics and massage.

Colonic irrigation and vaginal douches.

Mouth washes for treatment of periodontosis.

Emanatorium with hot air containing radon (inhalations).

Drinking cure with brine, iron, alkali, akaline earth, sulphur, iodine, Glauber salt, and peat waters.

Inhalation with natural steam from medicinal springs — either in separate inhalation rooms or by apparatus in separate booths.

Breathing exercises.

Kneipp hydrotherapy.

Health is the vital principle of bliss

— *Thomson*

Health Spas of Switzerland

There are 21 spas in Switzerland offering very nearly all possible cures. There are also some 40 different climatic regions designated by the Association of Swiss Climatic Health Resorts. (A climatic health resort can be any town or village that has a climate with therapeutic properties.)

The following list indicates which Swiss resorts are best suited for one's particular ailments, according to classification by the Medical Indications Committee of the Swiss Society for Balneology and Bioclimatology:

General debility: convalescence, disturbances during the climacteric and old age, vegetative neuroses, "executive's disease."

All Swiss spas are considered suitable for these generalized health disturbances. The choice of the spa should be made according to the constitution and age of the patient and the climatic factors (bracing or relaxing).

Chronic rheumatism: rheumatic diseases; deformities and

See also Pages 37-39.

degenerative conditions of the joints and vertebrae; arthritis, arthrosis, spondylosis; neuritis, neuralgia, sciatica; motor disturbances.

These diseases are treated at the following Swiss spas: *thermal baths* — Baden, Bad Ragaz-Pfafers, Loeche-les-Bains, Vals; *warm sulphur springs* — Lavey, Schinznach; *sulphur springs* — Heustrich, Lenk i. S., Rietbad, Schwefelbergbad, Stabio; *brine baths* — Bex, Rheinfelden; *radioactive baths* — Disentis; *peat and mud baths* — Acquarossa, Andeer, St. Moritz, Val Sinestra; *sand baths* — Lavey.

Paralysis: Baden, Bad Ragaz-Pfafers, Loeche-les-Bains, Schinznach, Vals (all have indoor thermal baths for exercise or swimming).

Heart diseases: Passugg, St. Moritz, Scuol-Tarasp-Vulpera, Vals Val Sinestra (natural carbonic acid baths).

Circulatory disorders: Baden, Bad Ragaz-Pfafers, Bex, Disentis, Lavey, Loeche-les-Bains, Passugg, Rheinfelden, Rietbad, St. Moritz, Schinznach, Scuol-Tarasp-Vulpera, Val Sinestra, Vals.

High blood pressure and the effects of *phlebitis:* the spas listed for heart diseases and circulatory disorders.

Stomach and intestinal disorders: Passugg, Rietbad, Scuol-Tarasp-Vulpera, Schinznach, Vals.

Diabetes: Passugg, Scuol-Tarasp-Vulpera, Schinznach.

Effects of tropical diseases: Passugg, St. Moritz, Scuol-Tarasp-Vulpera, Val Sinestra (arsenic springs).

Obesity (metabolic disorders), gout: Bad Ragaz-Pfafers, Passugg, Scuol-Tarasp-Vulpera, Vals.

Urinary problems: Bad Ragaz-Pfafers, Passugg, Rheinfelden, St. Moritz, Scuol-Tarasp-Vulpera.

Gynecological disorders: Andeer, Baden, Bex, Lavey, Loeche-les-Bains, Rheinfelden, St. Moritz.

Chronic catarrah and asthma (excluding tuberculosis): *sulphurous waters* (inhalation treatment) — Baden, Heustrich, Lavey, Lenki i. S., Rietbad, Schinznach, Schwefelbergbad, Sabio, Vals; *brine springs* (inhalation treatment) — Bex, Rheinfelden; *waters containing earths and salts* — Andeer.

Skin diseases: Acquarossa, Heustrich, Lavey, Lenk i. S., Loeche-les-Bains, Rietbad, Schinznach, Schwefelbergbad, Stabio, Val Sinestra.

Disorders of the gums (pyorrhea): Baden, Lenk i. S., St. Moritz, Schinznach.

Disorders of growth and development in childhood (glandular problems): Bex, Disentis, Lavey, Lenk i. S., Loeche-les-Bains, St. Moritz.

These are some contraindications suggested in Switzerland that probably apply to therapeutic bathing in general: severe or moderately severe cardiac disease, acute febrile conditions, tuberculosis, malignant growths, inflammatory rheumatism in an acute phase, acute phlebitis.

Health Spas of Italy

At this time we can do no more than list for the reader some of the spas in Italy:

Terme di S. Pellegrino, San Pellegrino Terme, Bergamo

Sorgente Sant'Elena, Viale Liberta' 112, 53042 Chianciano Terme, Siena

Societa' Napoletana Terme di Agnano, 80125 Agnano Terme, Napoli

Terme Demaniali di Acqui, Corso Bagni 2, 15011 Acqui Terme, Alessandria

Nuove Terme & Acqui Minerali, Via Cavour 1, 51016 Montecatini Terme, Pistoia

Ente Fiuggi, 03015 Fiuggi, Frosinone

Terme Stabiane, 80053 Castellamare di Stabia, Napoli

Terme di Recoaro, Via Roma 86, 36076 Recoaro Terme, Vicenza

Traditional bathing centers, modern institutes

Health Spas
of Bulgaria

More than 500 mineral waters springs in Bulgaria treat more than 250,000 Bulgarians and foreign visitors every year.

The health-giving virtues of *Hissar* lie in mineral springs that gush from the site of an extinct volcano. There have been bathing establishments here for 2,000 years.

The springs contain sodium, fluorine with a radon content, and some microelements such as copper, cobalt, and wolfram or tungsten. The waters are alkaline, hyperthermal, and hydrocarbonate, These mineral springs are said to relieve diseases of the urinary tract.

Many balneo-sanatoria and rest homes have been built in Hissar. Foreign visitors stay at the modern Augusta Sanatorium with accommodations for 160. There are excellent facilities for diagnosis and treatment; physiotherapeutic departments, rooms for massage and application of paraffin and for remedial gymnastics. Experienced doctors, specialists and a carefully trained medical staff look after the patients. Rates are among the lowest in Europe.

Bankya is only 10 miles from Sofia, capital of Bulgaria. It has a favorable climate and excellent mineral waters, High among the hills of the Lyulin Mountains, it is an ideal place for those in need of treatment and vacation.

The mineral waters of Bankya are hydrocarbonate, sulphate, and sodium of a low mineralization. They belong to the well-known Bulgarian alkaline waters, with a preponderance of carbonate and hydrocarbonic ions with traces of magnesium, iodine, and nitrogen.

Bankya is known for its balneo- (water therapy) sanatoria for adults and children, with more than 2,000 beds available, Doctors who specialize as clinicians, cardiologists, neurologists, and physiotherapists, and a great number of well-trained technicians furnish medical aid. The resort is under the guidance of the Institute for Postgraduate Specialization and Perfection of Doctors, Clinic of Rheumatology, and the Research Institute of Resort Study and Physiotherapy. Combined therapy is generally applied at the balneo-sanatoria. Side by side with balneo- and climatotherapy, every patient here may avail himself of electroheliotherapy, therapeutic gymnastics, terrain cure, massage, psychotherapy, and correct diet.

Bankya can be reached by trains leaving every 40 minutes from the central Sofia station and by buses every 15 minutes from the central bus stop in Sofia.

Kyustendil, known in antiquity as the "town of springs," is located on the slopes of Mount Ossogovo, some 60 miles from Sofia. It has 40 mineral springs whose waters are clear and colorless with an odor of sulphur due to its chemical composition.

The waters are used for rheumatism, arthritis, gynecological problems, disorders of the peripheral nervous system, and cardiovascular ailments.

. A large number of balnea-centers, sanatoria, and holiday

houses have been built in Kyustendil. On the outskirts of the town there is a special sanatorium for children.

Velingrad has 70 hot mineral springs and is surrounded by forests. Foreign visitors suffering from chronic, nonspecific inflammatory and allergic diseases of the lungs and respiratory system find relief here. Other ailments helped include bronchial asthma, goiter, secondary anemia, and arthritis.

Momin Prohod is a spa where treatments for metabolic and endocrine disorders, skin diseases, and polio are administered. Complex operations on the muscles, sinews, and bones are performed in the orthopedic departments.

Sofia Central Mineral Springs are hot springs used since Roman times. The waters are used for gastrointestinal disorders, gall bladder, liver, and kidney diseases.

Ovcha Koupel spa is half a mile from the center of Sofia. Its mineral waters treat functional ailments of the nervous system, the motor system, disturbed metabolism, and hypertension.

Knyazhevo spa is five miles from Sofia at the foot of Mount Vitosha. Its spring waters treat functional disorders of the nervous system, afflictions of the thyroid gland, obesity, and diabetes.

Gorna Banya spa is six miles from the center of Sofia. Water from its springs, bottled for sale abroad, contain sulphate, sodium, and potassium ions. The springs aid gastrointestinal disorders and liver and kidney disases.

Pancharevo spa is 10 miles from Sofia and has two hot springs. Their properties aid patients with chronic rheumatism, diseases of the joints and muscles and other arthritic suffers.

Further information and rates can be obtained and reservations made through the office of the Commerical Counselor to the Bulgarian Legation, 50 E. 42nd Street, Suite 1501, New York City, N. Y. 10036.

Personalized diets, gracious dining

Be timely wise;
With health all taste of pleasure flies

— Gay

Health Spas
of Yugoslavia

Yugoslavia has 87 spas, with 375 mineral springs that have been in use since 2,000 years ago when Roman soldiers occupied the region.

All of these spas and springs are in areas where the climate is excellent and they are usually surrounded by parks, woods, and forests. For this reason they have developed into tourist centers within easy reach of important historical and cultural monuments,

The spas are open year-round. They are well-organized and have modern health services with medical specialists in attendance. They offer current methods of diagnosis and treatment.

Most of them have modern hotels with central heating and there is also space available in private homes. Prices for lodging, food, and treatment are among the lowest in Europe.

Here are some of the most famous spas in Yugoslavia:

Bukovicka Banja-Arandjelovac is in the foothills of Mount Bukuljia in the central part of Sumadija, 50 miles from Belgrade. This is one of the most famous watering places in Serbia with a 100-year tradition of aiding sufferers of chronic liver ailments, stomach diseases, intestinal and urinary disorders, diabetes, and less severe forms of arterial hypertension. It has alkaline, carbonic acid water.

Cateske Toplice is in Slovenia on the right bank of the Sava River. It is 20 miles from Zagreb. The spa has a moderate subalpine climate with a Mediterranean influence. There are summer and winter olympic swimming pools with thermal waters of radioactive akrothothermal group. The spa deals with patients who are chronic rheumatism sufferers as well as with postorthopedic injury problems.

Daruvar, one of the most beautiful Slavonian towns, lies under the grape-growing Papuk slopes of the Toplica valley. Its hot mineral water springs serve to aid in female disorders including sterility, hormonal ailments, chronic rheumatic diseases, and conditions following gynecological operations.

Debarska Banja is located about 95 miles southwest of Skopje on the slopes of Mount Korab. Warm, sulphurous water as well as radioactive iron-sulphurous water is found here. Skin ailments, women's diseases, gastrointestinal problems, and rheumatism are treated, More than 450 beds are available in hotels and private homes.

Dobrna has radioactive, akrothermal mineral water used in chronic women's diseases, chronic inflammatory and degenerative rheumatism, "managerial" diseases, and various neurotic states. More than 600 beds are available at this spa in Slovenia, which is only 10 miles from Celije. There are railway connections with Ljubilijana, Zagreb, and Maribor.

Dolenjske Toplice is one of the larger spas with more than 1,700 beds available for patients suffering from chronic articular and muscular rheumatism, chronic women's diseases, climacteric states, and "managerial" diseases. It has an open-air swimming pool with the mineral waters having a temperature approximating human body temperature. The waters belong to the radioactive, akrothermal group.

Fojnica has a current capacity of more than 200 beds and is about 35 miles from Sarajevo. The spa has natural, radioactive water springs and treats chronic rheumatic diseases, consequences of wounds and injuries, sciatica, and other neuralgic ailments.

Igalo is located on the southern Adriatic on the shore of the most beautiful part of the Bay of Boka Kotorska, 15 miles from the Dubrovnik airport. The mineral waters are muriatic-saline. The health resort has 85 double bedrooms; and, in the vicinity, more than 2,000 additional beds available for patients. The shore at Igalo is flat and shallow which makes it convenient for patients and especially for children. The spa treats chronic inflammatory and degenerative rheumatism, posttraumatic states, postoperative states of the legs, chronic female diseases, and chronic problems of the respiratory organs.

Ilidza, 10 miles southwest of Sarajevo, treats chronic female disorders, postinjury conditions, sciatica, and other neuralgic conditions. More than 300 hotel rooms, all with hot mineral water of sulphurous-carbon-alkaline composition, are available at the spa. The resort is surrounded by the wooded slopes of Mount Igman.

Katlanovska Banja spa is 15 miles south of Skopje, in Macedonia beside the Pcinja River. The resort treats rheumatic and urological diseases, gastrointestinal tract ailments, and female sterility. More than 500 beds are available and two kinds of mineral waters: alkaline and alkaline-earth, and carbonic acid and sulphurous waters. The spa has a dense pine forest.

Koviljaca spa is 90 miles from Belgrade on the banks of the Drina River, in one of the largest wooded parks in Serbia. The resort helps patients with gynecological diseases, consequences of shock and war wounds, chronic inflammatory and degenerative rheumatism. More than 300 beds are available in nearby hotels and villas. The climate is mild and pleasant due to the nearby mountains, rivers, and woods.

Krapinske Toplice spa is 30 miles north of Zagreb in a wooded valley surrounded by hills. The spa contains four radioactive thermal springs and can accommodate more than 700 patients. It has an indoor swimming pool and sauna. The spa treats rheumatic diseases, postinjury of joints, muscles, bones, and nerves, chronic women's ailments, and general nerve problems.

Lipik spa has alkaline, muriatic water and treats chronic rheumatism, chronic cardiovascular diseases and ailments of the digestive organs. The climate is moderate and there are 150 beds available at the Hotel Begovaca.

Mataruska Banja spa is on the bank of the Ibar River near Kraljevo, about 110 miles south of Belgrade. More than 350 beds are available to patients suffering from deterioration of muscles, joints, bones, and nerves, inflammatory and degenerative diseases of the joints, female ailments (chronic inflammation and sterility). The mineral water of Mataruska Banja is sulphurous in nature.

Niska Banja spa has more than 850 beds available within a five-mile radius for patients who need help with inflammatory and degenerative rheumatism, chronic heart and blood vessel diseases, and gout. The springs of the spa belong to the radioactive group and are alkaline-earth in character.

Slatina Radenci spa is close to the Austria-Yugoslav border. More than 300 beds are available for patients suffering from cardiovascular diseases, digestive organ ailments, and urinary tract and "managerial" disorders. The open-air Olympic swimming pool and the large parks make it ideal for guests who come for vacations, preventive treatment, and summer holidays.

Rogaska Slatina spa in Slovenia has three mineral water springs composed of saline, alkaline, valley-alkaline, and carbonic acid elements. Ailments treated here are diseases of the digestive organs (inflammation of the stomach and intestines, gastric ulcer, chronic hepatitis, and conditions after hepatitis), chronic urological and cardiovascular diseases, and diabetes. More than 1,000 beds are available here in various hotels.

Sokobanja spa is located in the central part of eastern Serbia with some hot, radioactive springs in and around the grounds. Some 400 beds are available for sufferers from bronchial asthma, chronic rheumatism, arthritis, chronic female diseases, and sciatica.

Guber-Srebremica spa is in eastern Bosnia with about 25 diverse mineral springs. The three hotels can accommodate some 180 people. The spa treats some forms of anemia, neurological ailments, and convalescents.

Stubicke Toplice spa is located at the foot of Mount Zagrebacka Gora, about 25 miles from Zagreb. Two winter swimming pools with thermal, radioactive water are part of the rehabilitation center which specializes in medical care of injured and other ailing people.

There are five radioactive and hyperthermal springs. Mineral water preparations are also used. Ailments helped are rheumatism, postpolio conditions, and posttraumatic conditions. About 140 beds are available.

Vranjska Banja spa is surrounded by wooded hills and is convenient for rest treatment and recreation. The water is faintly sulphurous and hypothermal saline in composition. It can be used for bathing as well as drinking. These are the warmest mineral water springs in Yugoslavia. There are three hotels with approximately 400 rooms (heated by mineral water) for use by persons seeking relief from diseases affecting locomotion, chronic rheumatism, chronic women's diseases including sterility, and patients recovering from all types of injuries.

Information about Yugoslavian spas as well as all other data about travel in Yugoslavia can be obtained from the following tourist representatives:

Yugoslav National Tourist Office, 143 Regent Street, N. W. 1, London, England; and 509 Madison Avenue, New York N.Y. 10022

Office of Tourisme Yugoslave, 3, Rue de la Chaussée D'Antin, 9E, Paris, France.

Yugoslav Tourist Information Bureau, 4 Voukourestion Street, Athens, Greece.

Ufficion del Tourismo Jugoslavo, Via del Tritone 62, Rome, Italy 00187.

Health Spas of Finland

The spas listed here, 17 of them, are for the most part in southern Finland. The crisp Finnish climate is excellent for one's health. These spas operate as boarding establishments while also providing various kinds of health baths, nature treatments, and other forms of physical therapy. The services, treatments, and facilities offered by each establishment are listed separately. We strongly suggest that you write for reservations before you travel there.

Prices usually include room and board and treatments, with discounts for children and groups or families. However, some places charge extra for treatments and meals.

In Alavus
    Name of spa: Pieksulan Kesakoti
    Postal address: Alavus kk.
    Nearest railway station: Alavus; nearest bus station:
    Alavus
    Treatment: massage, clay compress
    Facilities: sauna, swimming pool
    Season: June-August
In Lisalmi
    Name of spa: Runnin Lomakylpyla
    Postal address: Runnin
    Nearest railway station: Runnin; nearest bus station:
        Lisalmi; Airport: Kuopio
    Treatment: massage, carbon and menthol baths, pine
        needle baths, clay compress, facial compact, ultraviolet
        treatments. Recommended for treatment of rheumatic
        ailments.
    Season: all year
In Ikaalinen
    Name of spa: Ikaalisten Kylpyla-Kuntoutuslaitos
    Postal address: Ikaalinen 2
    Nearest railway station: Tampere; nearest bus station:
        Ikaalinen
    Treatment: back stretching, neck stretching, infrared,
        carbon bath, foam bath, clay compresses, foam and pine
        needle baths, vapor bath.
    Facilities: swimming pool, game room, sauna, TV, lectures
    Season: all year
In Jamsankoski
    Name of spa: Lomahotelli Mon Repos
    Postal address: Koskenpaa
    Nearest railway station: Petajavesi; bus station: Kosken-
        paa; airport: Jyvaskyla
    Treatment: massage, clay and glycerine treatment, fluorine
        and pine needle baths
    Facilities: Swimming hall, swimming pool, lakeside sauna,
        TV, lounges
    Season: all year

In Lahti

Name of spa: Luontaishoitola Kauko Juntunen
Postal address: Lahti, Jalkaranta
Nearest railway station: Lahti; bus station, Lahti; airport: Seutula
Treatment: compresses and baths
Facilities: lakeside sauna, swimming, boating, TV, lounge
Season: all year

In Lappeenranta

Name of spa: Lappeenranta Kaupungin Klypylaitos
Postal address: Lappeenranta, Ainonkatu 17
Nearest railway station: Lappeenranta; bus station and airport: Lappeenranta
Treatments: formic acid bath, carbon bath, undulation treatment, galvanic, faradic and high-tension treatment, sauna, and ultraviolet radiation

In Lempaala

Name of spa: Lempaalan Luonnonparantola
Postal address: Lempaala
Railway and bus station: Lempaala; airport: Tampere
Treatment: clay and water compresses, massage, sauna
Facilities: sauna, reading room, boats, games
Season: all year

In Paimio

Name of spa: Paimion Klypylaitos
Railway and bus station: Paimio; airport: Turku
Treatment: clay and water compresses, massage
Facilities: sauna, swimming pool, radio, TV
Season: June-September

In Pello

Name of spa: Napariirin Luontaishoitola O/Y Korpikoti
Postal address: Turtola
Nearest railway station and bus station: Tornia; nearest airport: Kemi
Treatment: clay compresses, massage, vapor bath, oil cure
Facilities: sauna, bathing beach, radio, TV, library
Season: all year

In Pietarsaari
  Name of spa: AB Faboda Oy
  Season: June 20 to August 15

In Piikkio:
  Name of spa: Kiiskisen Luontaisparantola
  Nearest railway and bus station: Piikkio; airport: Turku
  Treatment: baths, clay treatment, steam, compresses, joint
    treatment
  Facilities: sauna, spa, swimming pools, TV
  Season: all year

In Piikkio:
  Name of spa: Toivonlinnan Kylpyarantola
  Postal address: Toivonlinnan, Piikkio
  Nearest railway station: Piikkio, bus and airport: Turku
  Treatment: baths, massage, heat treatment, light cures,
    electric treatment, diets. The spa has its own doctor.
  Facilities: sauna, separate swimming pools for men and
    women
  Season: June 9 to August 25

In Pyharanta:
  Name of spa: Pyharannan Merikylpyla
  Nearest railway stations: Uusikaupunki and Rauna;
    nearest bus station: Pyharanta; airport: Turku
  Treatment: massage, clay compresses, cold compresses
  Facilities: sauna, bathing beach, boats, TV, radio, piano
  Season: all year

In Savonlinna
  Name of spa: Savonlinnan Kylpyla
  Postal address: Savonlinna
  Nearest railway and bus station: Savonlinna
  Treatment: carbonate bath, salve bath, clay treatment,
    vibration massage, neck stretching, electrical stimula-
    tion, heat treatment, respiratory treatment
  Season: all year

In Sipoo
  Name of spa: Soderkullan Terveyskoti Oy
  Postal address: Kallback

Nearest railway and bus stations: Helsinki; nearest airport: Seutula

Treatment: hip baths, clay compresses, oil cures, diets, fasts, massage

Facilities: sauna and sauna lake

Season: all year

In Vihti

Name of spa: Hopeaniemen Kylpyarantola

Postal address: Nummela

Nearest railway and bus stations: Nummela; nearest airport: Seutula

Treatment: massage, physiotherapy, hot compresses, light cures, various baths

Facilities: lakeside sauna, TV, boats, games

Season: all year

In Vihti

Name of spa: Paivolan Kylpyparantola

Postal address: Vihti Nummela

Nearest railway and bus stations: Nummela; nearest airport: Seutula

Treatment: various baths and massage in the summer

Facilities: sauna, TV

Season: all year

Hot springs at Tiberias, near Galilee

The doctor of today
will be the dietician of tomorrow

— Alexis Carrel

Health Spas
of Israel

Probably the oldest spa in the world is at the hot springs of Tiberias, in Israel. The earliest reference to these springs is in the Bible (Joshua 19:35) where for the first time a settlement in this place is mentioned using the Hebrew word for hot springs, "Chamat" or "Hammath."

The springs contain sodium, calcium chloride, magnesium, and sulphur ions. The classification of the Tiberias springs is thermal-radioactive, with sulphurated, sodium, calcium, and chloride waters.

These springs help patients with ailments of the ambulatory system, nervous disorders, spinal and muscular trouble.

Patients with skin diseases such as psoriasis, neurodermatitis, and chronic eczema find in the hot springs at least temporary improvement.

At the opposite end of Israel, the ailing come from all over the world for relief in the hot mineral springs at the

Dead Sea. These are located between Zohar and Ein Bokek in the Negev, in the southern part of Israel.

The high concentration of minerals in these waters is valuable for the treatment of muscular stiffness, rheumatism, and for many skin diseases.

An additional therapeutic agent of some importance is the mud or clay on the shores of the Dead Sea. This is beneficial in the treatment of rheumatic and postparalytic illnesses. It also contains many minerals beneficial in the treatment of gynecological ailments.

The town of Arad, because of its desert location, height, dry air, and lack of vegetation, offers a unique combination of benefits to sufferers from asthma, allergies, and respiratory complaints.

The two most important springs in the area whose waters are being used for therapeutic purposes are those at Zohar and Ein Yesha. Both these springs are for bathing and not for drinking. They are classified as thermal-radioactive sulphur springs. The high magnesium content is a special property of this water, which is to be found in few other mineral springs. The presence of radon and radium make them the only radioactive springs presently in use in Israel. Because of their high mineral content, the waters of the Zohar hot springs are said to exert pressure on the arteries and muscles, improve blood circulation, and cleanse the body of wastes.

Ein Yesha hot spring is located a few miles south of Ein Gedi, only 150 feet or so from the seashore, and is richer in its sulphur content than the Zohar springs.

Ein Nott mineral spring waters are in use for drinking. They erupt from a slight slope about 650 feet from the shore. Dr. Moshe Atlas, Israel's leading balneologist, and former director of the spa at Bardejev, Czechoslovakia, has conducted studies that suggest that the springs help senior citizens reduce their cholesterol content significantly after drinking the waters daily for two weeks.

Hotels in Ein Bokek include: Galei Zohar Hotel facing the Dead Sea near the bathing beach. It has 115 double rooms.

Ein Bokek Hotel also faces the bathing beach and has 96 double rooms.

Hotels in Arad include: Masada Hotel, on an elevation overlooking the Dead Sea, with 50 double rooms. Margoa Hotel in the same location, has 80 double rooms in 10 separate buildings.

There are also hotels in Zohar, Masada, Ein Gedi, and Arad.

Persons wishing to take treatments in the Dead Sea area should make their hotel booking either directly with the hotel of their choice or through a travel agent. They should bring with them a medical report from their own doctor which can be presented to the doctor at the Zohar springs who will then prescribe the course of treatment.

It is not advisable for persons suffering from certain types of asthma to go down to the level of the Dead Sea. Asthma patients wishing to visit the Dead Sea should obtain medical advise as to whether it is preferable for them to book accommodation in Ein Bokek (some 200 feet below sea level) or in Arad (some 2,000 feet above sea level).

Your travel agent can make all necessary arrangements for transportation and accommodation.

Health and cheerfulness
Mutually beget each other

— Addison

Health Spas
of Japan

There are more than 90 designated hot springs in Japan
and we can do little more than list them for your convenience
and interest.

Spas in Hokkaido

Jozankei; Yunokawa, near Hakodate; *Noboribetsu; Karu-*
rusa, north of Noboribetsu spa; *Toyako,* southwestern shore
of Lake Toya; *Sounkyo,* in Daisetsuzan National Park in the
center Hokkaido; *Kawayu,* in Akan National Park near Lake
Mashu; *Onneyu,* Rubeshibe-cho, Abashiri.

Spas in Honshu

In Aomori prefecture — *Asamushi, Owani;* Iwate pre-
fecture — *Hanamaki;* Miyagi prefecture — *Sakunami, Narugo;*
Akita prefecture — *Otaki;* Yamagata prefecture — *Otaki;*
Yamagata prefecture — *Zao Kaminoyama, Akayu, Atsumi,*
Semi.

In Fukushima prefecture — *Tsuchiyu, Iizaka, Shinobu-*
Takayu, Higashiyama; in Niigata prefecture — *Yudanaka,*

Shibu, Asama, Kamisuwa, Tateshina; in Gumma prefecture — *Ikaho, Kusatsu, Minakami;* in Tochigi prefecture — *Nikko Yumoto, Kinugawa, Kawaji, Shiobara, Nasu.*

In Hakone — *Yumoto, Tonosawa, Miyanoshita, Gora, Sengokuhara, Kowakidani, Ashinoyu, Yunohanazawa, Yugawara, Atami, Izusan, Ajiro.*

In Izu peninsula — *Ito, Katase, Nirayama, Nagaoka, Ohita, Shuzenji, Shimoda, Toi.*

In Gifu prefecture — *Gero;* in Fukui prefecture — *Awara;* in Ishikawa prefecture — *Yamanaka, Katayamazu, Yamashiro, Awazu, Wagura;* in Toyama prefecture—*Unazuki, Yunoyama.*

In Kyoto — *Kizu;* in Wakayama prefecture — *Shirahama, Katsuura;* in Hyogo prefecture — *Takarazuka, Arima, Kinosaki.*

Okayama prefecture — *Okutsu, Yunogo;* in Yamaguchi prefecture — *Yuda;* in Tottori prefecture — *Kaike, Misasa;* in Shimane prefecture — *Tamatsukuri.*

Spas on Skikoku Island

In Ehime prefecture — *Dogo.*

Spas in Kyushu

In Fukuoka prefecture — *Futsukaichi, Harazuru;* in Nagasaki prefecture — *Unzen, Obama;* in Kumamoto prefecture — *Aso, Yunoko, Tsuetate.*

In Oita prefecture — *Beppu, Amagase;* in Saga prefecture *Ureshino;* in Kagoshima prefecture — *Kirishima, Ibusuki.*

Part IV
Some Special Information

Special treatments for special needs

Nor love, nor honour, wealth or pow'r
Can give the heart a cheerful hour
When health is lost.

— Gay

Who Treats What?

Ailments and the spas and resorts where they are treated

Heart and circulatory ailments

West Germany

Bad Pyrmont   Aix-la-Chapelle   Baden-Baden
Tolz   Bad Homburg   Bad Nauheim
                    Bad Marienburg

East Germany

Bad Brambach   Bad Liebenstein   Bad Elster

Switzerland

St. Moritz   Bircher-Benner Clinic   Passugg
Vals

Czechoslovakia

Nad Becvov   Frantiskovy   Sliac
Jachymov   Konstantinovy Lazne Beloves
                    Podebrady

Bulgaria

Kyustendil

Eye ailments

Austria

Bad Hall

West Germany

Durrheim	Rothenfelde	Wiessee

Skin diseases

Austria

Bad Burgwies	Bad Deutsch Altenburg	Baden
Heilbrunn	Schwefelbad Hohenems	Bad Haering
Vienna-Pfannsches	Bad St. Leonhard	Mitteandorf
Mineral	Woerschach	Bad Weinberg
	Schwelfelbad	

West Germany

Aachen	Langenbrucken	Abbach
Nenndorf	Eilsen Mingolsheim	Durkheim
Senkelteich	Buchinger Sanatorium	Wiessee
Bad Pyrmont		

East Germany

Heiligendamm

Czechoslovakia

Lipova	Marianske Lazne	Smrdaky

Bulgaria

Momin Prohod

Israel

Tiberias Hot Springs	Ein Bokek

Mexico

Rio Caliente	Villa Vegetariana	Topo Chico

Switzerland

Acquarossa	Bircher-Benner Clinic	Lenk
Rietbad	Schwefelbergbad	Lavey
Stabio	Loeche-les-Bains	Val Sinestra
	Schwinznach	

Great Britain

Champney's	Ingelery Hydro Health Clinic

United States

Meadowlark	Hidden Valley Health Ranch

Rheumatism and diseases of the joints

West Germany

Aachen	Buchinger Sanatorium	Aibling
Bramstadt	Baden-Baden	Essen
Heidelberg	Bad Pyrmont	Steinbeck
Abbach	Bad Nenndorf	Steben
Driburg		Orb

East Germany

Berggiesshubel	Heiligendamm Sanatorium
Bad Brambach	Bad Elster

Czechoslovakia

Piestany	Trencianske Teplice	Dudince
Trebon	Frantiskovy Lazne	Bohdanec
Bojnice	Velichovky	Darkov

Switzerland

Baden	Bad Ragaz-Pfafers	Lavey
St. Moritz	Val Sinestra	B E X

Israel

Nve Zohar	Tiberias Hot Springs

England

Champney's	Cheltenham Spa	Bath
Droitwich	Royal Leamington Spa	Enton Hall

Bulgaria

Bankya	Pancharevo	Velingrad
Kyustendil	Ovcha Koupel	

France

Vichy	Aix-les-Bains

Mexico

Topo Chico Spa	Villa Vegetariana	Rio Caliente

Russia

Odessa	Kislovdsk	Yalta
Sochi		

United States

Palm Springs	Desert Hot Springs	Hot Springs

Metabolic diseases including diabetes, gout, and obesity

West Germany

Ingelfingen	Wiesbaden	Daun
Hersfeld	Bodendorf	Seebruch
Landsthul	Bad Homburg	Melle
Kissingen	Aix-la-Chapelle	Boll
Steinbeck	Badenweiler	Ritenau
Krozingen	Mergentheim	Honnef
Neuenahr	Stuttgart-Cannstatt	Konig
Bentheim		

East Germany

Antonshohe	Berggiesshubel

Austria

Baden Near Vienna
Salzburg Therapeutic Center
Woerschach Schwefelbad
Velden Am Woerschach
Tuffbad bei St. Lorenzen
Warmbad Villach
Schwefelbad Hohenems

Gmunden
Bad Gleichenberg
Bad Schoenau
Bad Haering
Schruns
Gallspach
Seefeld

Czechoslovakia

Korytnica
Luhacovice
Jachymov

Karlovy Vary (Carlsbad)
Frantiskovy Lazne
Marianske Lazne
Novy Smokovec

Lucky
Jesenik
Lipova

Bulgaria

Ovcha Koupel

Sofia Mineral Baths

Bankya

Switzerland

Lavey
Rietbad
Acquarossa
Val Sinestra
Heustrich

Bircher-Benner Clinic
Bad Ragaz-Pfafers
Loeche-les-Bains
Schwefelberg Bad
Schwinznach

Baden
St. Moritz
Bex
Lenk
Stabio

England

Tyringham Clinic
Middleton Stoney
Champney's

Nature-Cure Clinic
Weymouth Hydro

Bath
Enton Hall

Israel

Tiberias Hot Springs Ein Noit Mineral Springs Ein Bokek

Cancer

Mexico

Hoxey Clinic

Pan-American Clinic

West Germany

Ringberg Clinic   Buchinger Sanatorium

United States

Dr. Evers Hospital   Byron W. Goldberg, D.O.

Female disorders

Czechoslovakia

Lucky   Frantiskovy Lazne

Austria

Moorbad Reuthe   Salzburg Therapeutic Center
Salzerbad   Moorbad Neydharting   Bad Schoenau

England

Tyringham   Naturopathic Private Clinic
Champney's   for Women
Enton Hall

East Germany

Bad Elster   Bad Brambach

West Germany

Bad Homburg   Bad Mergentheim   Bad Grund
Bad Pyrmont   Buchinger Sanatorium   Bad Bertrich
Bad Neuenahr   Bad Kreuznach   Badenweiler

Bulgaria

Kyustendil

Israel

Tiberias Hot Springs

Liver and gall bladder, stomach and intestinal complaints

Switzerland

Rheinfelden	Bircher-Benner Clinic	Rietbad
Valsinestra	Passugg	Vulpera
Tarasp		

Czechoslovakia

Marianske Lazne	Karlovy Vary (Carlsbad)	Luhacovice
(Marienbad)	Bardejovske Kupefe	

Mexico

Villa Vegetariana

Russia

Kislovdsk	Sochi-Matsesta

France

Aix-les-Bains	Aix-en-Provence	Vichy

United States

Shangri-La	Orange Grove Health Ranch

Austria

Bad Aussee	Bad Gleichenberg	Bad Ischl
Bad Gastein	Bad Deutsch Altenburg	

East Germany

Bad Elster	Potsdam Neufahrland

West Germany

Bad Homburg	Buchinger Sanatorium	Wiesbaden
Bad Neuenahr	Stuttgart-Canstatt	Kissingen
Driburg	Baden-Baden	

Bulgaria

Gorna Banya   Sofia Central Mineral   Hissar
                     Springs

Respiratory diseases

Austria

Aflenz   Bad Gleichenberg   Bad Aussee
Bad Aussee   Bad Gastein-Boeckstein   Bad Hall
Aflenz   Thermal Gallery   Bad Obladis
Bad Leonfelden   Salzburg Therapeutic   Semmering
Seefeld   Center   Bad Ischl

West Germany

Baden-Baden   Bad Lippspringe   Schwartau
Bad Durrheim   Reichenhall   Bad Nauheim
Bad Harzburg   Sooden-Allendorf   Bad Ems
Salzhausen   Bad Ganderersheim   Sassendorf
Badenweiler   Bad Kreuznach   Wimpfen

East Germany

Heiligendamm   Bad Salzungen   Bad Kosen

Czechoslovakia

Jesenik   Nimnica

Switzerland

Lausanne   Chateau d'Oex   Lenk
Locarno   Burgenstock   Zermatt
St. Moritz

France

Le Mont Dore   Aix-les-Bains

Children's diseases

West Germany

Salzhausen	Reichenhall	Essen
Kreuznach	Sassendorf	Munster
Luneburg	Rothenfelde	

Switzerland

Passugg	Scuol Tarasp	Locarno
St. Moritz	Val Sinestra	Rheinfelden
Lausanne	Bad Ragaz-Pfafers	Bex
Burgenstock	Loeche-les-Bains	Lenk
Rietbad	Chateau d'Oex	Heustrich
Vulpera	Schwefelberg Bad	Zermatt
Baden	Acquarossa	Stabio
Lavey	Schinznach	

Bulgaria

Velingrad	Momin Prohod	Bankya

Czechoslovakia

Podebrady	Frantiskovy Lazne	Cjz
Velke Losiny	Marianske Lazne	Smrdaky
Janske Lazne	Belohrad Bludov	Sliac
Luhacovice	Teplice Nad Becvou	Stos
Zeleznice	Karlovy Vary (Carlsbad)	Piestany
Darkov	Teplice v. Cechach	

France

Aix-les-Bains	Le Mont Dore	Vichy

Austria

Bad Aussee	Bad Ischl	Bad Hall
Salzer Bad	Salzburg Therapeutic Center	
Solbad Hall		

Fear less, hope more
Eat less, chew more
Whine less, breathe more
Hate less, love more
And all good things are yours

— Swedish proverb

Health Spa Terminology

Acidulous waters — slightly sour and acid.

Affusions — water is poured on the body or a part of it.

Akrothermal — very hot mineral waters.

Alkali — one of a class of bases, such as soda, that neutralize acids (forming salts with them).

Arthritis — inflammation of the joints.

Arteriosclerosis — fatty degeneration in the walls of the blood vessels, thickening of the walls with more or less hardening.

Asthma — (bronchial) — difficulty in breathing, due to a spasm of the muscle fibers in the walls of the smaller bronchial tubes or swelling of the membrane.

Autonomic nervous system — the involuntary nervous system.

Balneology — science of mineral waters and their healing powers.

Bile — secretion produced by the liver.

Bitumen — any one of various petroleum products.

Blood count — calculation of the number of red or white cells and other particles in a cubic millimeter of blood.

Bronchitis — inflammation of the bronchi (air passages in the lungs).

Buerger's disease — destructive inflammation of small blood vessels of the extremities, sometimes resulting in gangrene.

Bursitis — inflammation of a bursa, or pocket, in a joint cavity.

Calcium — a metallic element found in large quantities in the body; an essential ingredient in bones and teeth.

Capillaries — very minute, hair-like blood vessels.

Carbonic acid — a gaseous, colorless compound of carbon and oxygen

Carbon dioxide — product of the combustion of carbon; dissolves in water to form carbonic acid.

Cardiovascular — blood vessel structure of the heart.

Cartilage — elastic tissue, forming bone and gristle.

Cataract—a disease of the eye in which the crystalline lens becomes clouded, impairing vision.

Chalybeate — waters charged with iron.

Chiropractic — a system of therapeutic treatment of disease through the articulations (joints, junctures between bones) of the human body, particularly those of the spine with the object of relieving pressure or tension upon nerve filaments (fine threads).

Cholesterol — a clear, fatty alcohol found especially in blood, nerve tissue, bile, and in animal fats.

Chronic — of a prolonged or recurring nature.

Colitis — inflammation of the colon.

Cystitis — inflammation of the bladder.

Cytology — scientific study of the cells, their origin, structure, and function.

Dermatitis — inflammation of the skin.

Dermatology — scientific studies of the skin and its diseases.

Detoxification — cleansing of the body from toxins, poisonous substances produced by bacteria and other agents.

Diabetes mellitus — a metabolic disease, in which sugar is excreted in the urine due to lack of or inadequate utilization of insulin.

Diaphoretic — an agent that increases perspiration.

Diuretic — an agent that increases the flow of urine.

Dropsy — abnormal accumulation of serous (serum) fluid in the cellular tissue or in a body cavity.

Dyspnea — difficulty in breathing.

Eczema — an inflammation of the skin.

Edema — dropsy, a swelling.

Electrocardiogram — a recording of changes of electrical potential during the heart beat.

Electrolysis — a way of producing changes in the cells by the use of an electric current.

Emanatorium — room with hot vapor; inhaled to relieve respiratory congestion.

Embolism — obstruction of a blood vessel by a clot or other abnormal particle.

Emphysema — dilation of the lung leading to an insufficient aeration of the blood.

Endocarditis —- inflammation of the lining of the heart and its valves.

Enzyme — a substance that effects changes in the body without itself being substantially altered.

Etiology — study of the cause of disease.

Focus of infection — the main site of a general infection (septic focus).

Gauss therapy — a form of electrotherapy.

Glauber salt — a crystalline sodium salt used as a cathartic or purgative.

Gynecology — study of women's hygiene and diseases.

Heliotherapy — treatment with light, natural or artificial.

Hemoglobin — an iron compound in blood cells aiding in oxygenation of body tissues.

Herpes zoster (shingles) — acute nerve inflammation associated with eruption of blisters on the skin.

Histology — study of the minute structure and organization of tissues.

Homeopathy — a medical system which treats disease by the administration of minute quantities of medicines that would in healthy persons produce symptoms of the disease being treated.

Hydrocarbonate — a hydrogen carbonate, a biocarbonate, from hydrocarbon; an organic compound containing hydrogen and carbon, found in petroleum, natural gas, bitumens.

Hydrotherapy — treatment of a condition with the external application of water.

Hyperpyrexia — high fever, sometimes artificially induced as therapy.

Lavage — therapy involving the washing of an organ.

Lithium — a light metal occuring in combination in some mineral waters. Its salts are solvents of uric acid.

Metabolism — the processes in the body by which tissues are built up and destroyed in the production of energy.

"Managerial" disease — the particular combination of ailments attributable of sedentary, stressful work.

Mineral waters — waters containing mineral salts or gases.

Mucous membrane — delicate lining of the digestive, respiratory, and other passages of the body.

Muriatic waters — briny waters containing chlorides.

Myelitis — certain inflammations and softening of the spinal cord.

Nephritis — inflammation of the kidney.

Neurology — branch of medical science dealing with the nervous system.

Opthalmo-iontophoresis — introduction of medicinal materials to the eye, via ion transfer by application of an electric current.

Osteomalacia — softening of the bones because of deficiencies in minerals and vitamin D.

Kneipp cure — after Father Sebastian Kneipp (19th century), who developed various forms of hydrotherapy.

Osteopathy — a system of healing by manual therapuetics for the structural correction of tissue, in combination with other forms of therapy.

Parafango — application of mudcoating or packs.

Pathogenic — causing disease.

Pathology — the study of diseases.

Periodontosis — disease affecting gums and dental membranes.

Peristalsis — successive waves of contraction of the walls of the intestines or other passageways, moving the contents onward.

Prophylactic — helping to prevent disease.

Psammotherapy — the taking of sand baths as a remedial treatment.

Psoriasis — a chronic skin disease.

Psychotherapy — treatment designed to produce a response by mental rather than physical effects.

Ptosis — prolapse or dropping of an organ or part.

Purgative — cathartic, laxative.

Pyelitis — inflammation of the pelvis, or main cavity, of the kidney.

Pyretic — pertaining to a fever.

Radium — radioactive metallic element.

Radon — a gaseous, radioactive element produced by disintegration of radium.

Respiratory — relating to breathing.

Rheumatism — a condition marked by inflammation or pain in joints or muscles.

Sanatorium — an institution providing treatments, usually of a physical nature, together with diet, exercise and other procedures for recovery and rehabilitation.

Scotch mist — thick mist and drizzle.

Sedimentation — the deposit or settling of solid matter — as in urine that has been allowed to stand for some time.

Sinusoidal — relating to a blood channel in certain organs, such as the spleen, liver, and bone marrow.

Sodium — a metallic element of the alkali group, occurring in combination (the base of soda).

Spa — a health resort developed in association with one or more mineral springs, the waters of which possess therapeutic properties.

Sulfur — a yellow, nonmetallic element, insoluble in water, but occurring in mineral springs in various combinations with other elements.

Terrain therapy — treatment by the use of walkways of varied length and angle.

Thalassotherapy — treatment of disease in association with the sea, living close to the sea, bathing in the sea water, breathing sea air.

Therapeutics — dealing with the application of remedies for the cure of diseases.

Thermal — pertaining to heat or hot water or springs.

Toxins — poisonous substances produced by the metabolism of certain organisms.

Ultraviolet — invisible radiation with a wavelength shorter than the violet of the visible spectrum.

Urticaria — inflammatory skin disease or hives; often produced by an allergic reaction.

Vascular — pertaining to ducts and blood vessels.

They are as sick that surfeit with too much
As they that starve with nothing

— Shakespeare

Appendix

Some menus, recipes, and health tips from Meadowlark Health Spa, Hemet, California

Menus

Breakfast

Muesli (see recipes)
Whole grain toast
1 slice butter or safflower margarine
Apple butter (unsweetened) 1 teaspoon; or fresh fruit
Millet or oatmeal (steel ground)
An egg
Herb tea, milk, buttermilk, yogurt (If you can't leave coffee,
    use a decaffeinated type until you learn how.)
If in a hurry — Currier Cocktail (see recipes)

Lunch

Soup without flour thickening: clam chowder, tomato, beef-
barley, chicken or puree of vegetables added to milk
Fresh vegetable or fruit salad
Cheese (unprocessed) with crisp rye, or one slice whole grain
bread
Fresh fruit if desired
Herb tea

Dinner

Celery, olives, carrots, jicama sticks; or plate of raw, grated
beets, turnips, carrots and jicama to start meal
Meat, fish or foul (meat preferably not more than two to
three times a week). As a meat substitute use egg, cheese,
nut loaves, etc. Meat should be comparatively rare and
cooked at low temperature.
Two steamed or baked vegetables: one green, one yellow
Brown rice, spaghetti, or noodles (from sesame or artichoke
flour), or a
Fresh fruit if desired
Herb tea

Special foods and nutritional tips

Snacks if hypolglycemia is a problem

To be taken between meals — midmorning, midafternoon,
and bedtime — unless there is a diabetes or overweight
problem, then only at bedtime:
Unprocessed cheese with apple slices
Unroasted, unsalted nuts, if one is not overweight (a small
handful only): brazils, almonds, walnuts, sunflower seeds
Cottage cheese and fruit
Small glass buttermilk or raw milk
When raw foods become 50 to 60 percent of your diet your
in-between-meals feedings will become less necessary.

Desirable beverages

Herb teas, milk, buttermilk, soybean milk, fruit or vegetable juices — excepting prune or grape

Desserts

Fresh fruit, unsweetened substitute desserts, junket

Fruits

Apples, peaches, apricots, pears, berries, grapefruit, oranges, melons, pineapple, and all unsweetened fruits — except grapes and prunes

Vegetables

Asparagus, avocados, beets, broccoli, brussels sprouts, cabbage, cauliflower, carrots, corn, celery, cucumber, eggplant, lima beans, peas, radishes, onions, squash, string beans, green beans, zuccini
One small, crisply baked potato without center
Spaghetti and macaroni made with artichoke or sesame flour

Free foods — all you desire

Celery sticks, head lettuce — or redleaf or romaine
Bell peppers, mushrooms, and nuts — if not overweight

Foods to increase protein intake

Use frequently: protein concentrate drinks, brewer's yeast, millet meal, wheat germ (not toasted), and soybean preparations

Foods and practices to avoid

Sugars, honey, candy, cake, pie, pastries, sweetened custards, ice cream, and all other sweets
Some potatoes, white rice, grapes, raisins, plums, figs, and dates

White-flour spaghetti, macaroni, noodles
Caffeine — coffee, tea, cola drinks and low calorie cola drinks
All alcoholic beverages
Do not use aluminum cooking utensils or aluminum wrapping
　　foil
Use less salt

Some Meadowlark recipes

Muesli

2 tablespoons oats, granola, or other whole grain cereal soaked
　　overnight in ¼ cup unsweetened pineapple juice
In morning, add ½ apple or other fruit, ½ banana, and nuts
Put through grinder and serve
Serves two

Muesli Supreme

2 tablespoons cooked oats or millet. Add fruit and nuts cut
　　in pieces: ½ orange, ½ apple, 1 tablespoon raisins, 2 table-
　　spoons fresh pineapple, 6 almonds, 4 walnut halves
Add 2 tablespoons sunflower seeds and ½ cup low-fat milk
　　if desired

Chicken-Barley Soup

1 medium frying chicken　　1 cup sliced celery
½ cup barley (whole)　　1 cup chopped onion
1 cup sliced carrots
Cook chicken 45 minutes. Add vegetables and season to taste.
　　Cook ½ hour. Add 1 cup zuccinni during the last 15
　　minutes.

Mushroon-Barley Soup

½ cup barley (whole)
8 cups water
Cook the barley in 2 cups water until tender
In 6 cups water, cook: ½ cup diced carrots, ½ cup diced celery
　　root, ½ cup diced parsnips, ¼ cup chopped onions.
When vegetables are cooked, take out 2 cups broth and 1
　　cup vegetables. Put this in blender and add: ½ tablespoon

salt, ¹/₂ tablespoon sweet basil, 1 tablespoon chopped
parsley, 1 tablespoon cashew nuts, 1 clove garlic. Liquefy
and add to soup.
Add cooked barley and one cup chopped, fresh mushrooms.
Simmer slowly, stirring constantly. Serve hot with chopped
parsley on top.

Currier Cocktail

1 or 2 glasses nonfat milk; 1 or 2 eggs; 1 or 2 eggs; 1 or 2
tablespoons powdered milk (skim); 1 tablespoon primary
food yeast or brewer's, such as Torumel; 1 tablespoon
each of wheat germ or rice polishings; lecithin granules;
powdered liver protein; cold-pressed safflower, or corn oil.
Blend by hand or electric mixer. Flavor if desired. Refrigerate.

Salads

Alternate slices of grapefruit and avocado on lettuce leaves.
Sprinkle with toasted wheat germ

Sunflower Seed Loaf

1¹/₂ cups ground sunflower seeds	2 eggs, beaten slightly
³/₄ cups ground sesame seed meal	1 tablespoon apple cider
¹/₂ cup chopped nuts (walnuts)	vinegar
1 cup cooked lentils	¹/₂ cup diced celery
¹/₂ cup grated raw beets	1 cup whole grain flour
3 tablespoons chopped chives	2 tablespoons lemon juice

Blend together all ingredients, press into oiled baking dish.
Bake until done — about 40 minutes at 325°. Serve hot
with raw salad — one-half fresh pear filled with grated
cheese and sour cream.

Starch-free Cookies

1 cup chopped walnuts	¹/₂ cup honey
4 egg whites	1 cup dry cereal
¹/₈ pound butter	

Beat egg whites until stiff. Mix all dry ingredients individually.
Fold in egg whites. Drop by teaspoons onto hot, oiled cookie
sheet and bake at 350° for 20 minutes.

BiRCHer / Benner =
3 mil — cts
6 yr Course — med. Student

Typography: Friedrich Typography
Santa Barbara, California

Printing and Binding:
Griffin Printing and Lithograph
Glendale, California